The Art of World Travel
The Ultimate Guide To Freedom, Adventure And Living An Epic Life

Justin Troupe

Copyright © 2014 Justin Troupe
All rights reserved.

ISBN: 0692026711
ISBN 13: 9780692026717

Introduction   v

PART ONE:

THE ART OF TRAVEL   1
Igniting Your Travel Dreams   3
Facing Fear, Smashing Excuses   15
Craft a Compelling Travel Action Plan   27
Clearing the Path: Fear and the Time Vampires   33
Your Travel Dream Team   39
Wrangling the Details to Freedom   47

PART TWO:

THE ULTIMATE TRAVEL HACKING GUIDE   53
Introduction   55
Old-school Approach: Bartering for travel   57
The New Approach: Hacking the Airline Points System!   59
How to Get Unlimited Free Airline Tickets   62
Making Airlines Work for You: The Stack-Your-Miles Strategy   70
The Ultimate Endless Weekend: Buying Your First RTW Airline Ticket   76
A Simple Guide to Amazing Accommodations: How to book mind-blowing places all over the world for the lowest price!   85
Amazing Tour companies and interesting travel discount websites   97
Cutting Edge TRAVEL GEAR   102
10 Secrets to Surviving 24 Hours of Flying   112
Location-Independent Nomads: Hacking the World Using Global Arbitrage   119
The Secret Facebook Hack You Need to Know   130

How to Avoid Getting Sick, Frustrated or Burned Out on a
Long Travel Stint   134
Open Your Heart, Give Back to the World   140

Introduction

---

*[This is] the most dangerous risk of all. The risk of
spending your life not doing what you want on the bet
you can buy yourself the freedom to do it later.*
– Randy Komisar

You are about to learn the black arts of travel. After reading this book, you will be able to fly virtually anywhere you can imagine for free, stay in mansions or condos for nothing, and even plan your first trip around the world. You will have a travel vision you're excited about, and know exactly how to make it happen. I am also including a small library of state-of-the-art gadgets, websites and products so you can easily adapt to new and exotic locations.

Any travel dream you can imagine is now within your reach.

Welcome to the master class for your bucket list.

I've spent most of the last ten years selling various travel products and talking to thousands of people about their dreams. Because most people need a travel vision and concrete plans just as much as the "how to" advice, I'm including a foolproof system for reaching your travel goals. I discovered that almost everyone has the same challenges, so the first section of the book will help you deal with anything holding you back from your travel dreams.

This book has two parts:

Part One will help you uncover your travel vision and learn tools to overcome virtually every excuse that has held you back, such as fear or doubt. It will also introduce you to a new movement of people living a completely mobile lifestyle, many of whom have visited between 100 to 200 countries.

Completing the first part of this book will ensure that you never end up being one of the many people who have given up on their travel dreams due to day-to-day pressures such as finances, schedules and family responsibilities.

Part One will help you reconnect with your deepest reasons to travel and amplify them until find yourself on a plane having your wildest travel fantasies come true.

Yes, I said fantasies! If you going to manifest the trip of a lifetime it starts by picking whatever dream lights your fire.

You may be surprised how easy this will be for you. Most people go to college, plan weddings, buy houses, and raise children. All of these tasks are far more difficult than charting your first trip around the world - let alone a few weeks traveling through Europe or Asia!

Part Two is the master class on how to make your vision straightforward and affordable. With a bit of imagination, there are countless ways to see the world, and many of them are free or even allow you to make money on the road.

Completing Part Two will help you do things like earn one million frequent flyer miles in six months or stay in a free villa in Italy for three weeks. It will also give you the tools needed for round-the-world vacations that last for months or even years.

Most of us never seriously entertain the idea that we can quit our jobs and take a year or two off to travel. Many people also can't imagine a world where you can travel as long as you want, moving from country to country on a whim. This kind of lifestyle is not only possible, but is reality for hundreds of thousands of people who live a location-independent life right now. Thousands more join every day. You can, too.

The biggest misconception about long-term travel is that it's only for college kids who want to backpack. These days, it's not only college kids, but people of all ages and even entire families enjoying a mobile lifestyle.

The last couple of chapters will cover some timeless secrets on how to easily create gratitude and joy and more deeply connect to the present moment. This awareness will not only help you enjoy the places you visit, but it will also change the entire path of your trip.

Many of the greatest adventures in life will come from the people you meet while you are traveling. If you are happy, grateful and present, people will connect with you, and when they do, their advice and connections will change the entire path of your trip.

For those of you who already ridiculously motivated to travel, you can feel free to skip to the practical section.

As for everyone else, I hope you will grab a pen and plan the biggest adventure of your life. By using just part of the information inside these pages, you can have any travel dream you've ever imagined.

Please enjoy, and I hope to see you out on the road –

Justin

Part One:

The Art Of Travel

one

Igniting Your Travel Dreams

People say that what we're all seeking is a meaning for life. I don't think that's what we're really seeking. I think what we're seeking is an experience of being alive, so that our life experiences on the purely physical plane will have resonance within our own innermost being and reality, so that we actually feel the rapture of being alive.
– Joseph Campbell

I have always admired people who travel. I'm not talking about the ones who take an occasional family vacation, but people who set out to see everything, people who seem to live fearlessly, and people who experience one incredible adventure after the other.

A Leap Of Faith

My own crazy adventure started right out of high school. Immediately after my eighteenth birthday, I got jumped on a plane and moved to the Caribbean with exactly $274 in my pocket. I slept under the stars on an incredible beach for almost a month until I got a job and a place to live.

Why?

I just found out I was going to die in less than six months.

Well, sort of. In my senior year of high school, I was disillusioned with school and hated the Idaho town where I was living. I was hanging out with the wrong people and was one mistake away from landing myself in very serious trouble. I had one teacher with a Ph.D. in philosophy who challenged me to write a paper on what would do if I had only six months left to live. I genuinely liked the teacher, and writing the paper made me think about what was it I really wanted out of my life.

The first thing on my list was a plan to run away and live in the Caribbean. I had this gut level feeling that I needed to make this happen now or I would never do it. Over several months, with a part-time job, I saved enough money to buy an airline ticket to the Virgin Islands. At the last minute, my savings took a hit, and I was left with $274 to my name.

What would you do if presented with such a decision? Would you listen to people who were telling you that you were crazy – which was basically everyone? Or would you trust your dream and just go for it?

I decided that my dream couldn't wait. I got on the plane, without a job or a place to stay. I didn't know anyone. On the plane over, I was scared and excited at the same time. After landing, I asked a taxi driver to take me to the closest beach. I hiked around half a mile and found a place that looked deserted to set up camp. The water was crystal clear and a massive hillside of jungle rose up behind me. I stashed my things in the jungle and slept right there in a sleeping bag between two palm trees.

Imagine sleeping on a beach for your first night thousands of miles from home on a Caribbean island. There was almost zero light pollution on the beach and the stars were brilliantly clear. All through the night, the sound of the waves lulled me to sleep. Waking up to the sunrise and the feeling of the trade winds kissing my face was simply amazing. However, it was more than just being someplace beautiful. It was one of those moments when a sense of excitement and possibility that ripples through your mind – moments when you realize at a deep level that anything is possible.

*I can't think of anything that excites a greater sense
of childlike wonder than to be in a country where
you are ignorant of almost everything.*
  – *Bill Bryson*

Three weeks into my adventure, things were getting difficult. I had less than $100 and was running low on options. At the suggestion of a random person I met, I walked into a Catholic church and started talking to a priest. I explained my situation and mentioned where I was camping. He was quite worried that I was sleeping on a beach, and after talking to me for about ten minutes he made two phone calls.

The first one was to a lady in his church who had a house that was being rebuilt. The first floor was fine, but the top floor had been damaged by a hurricane, and was being rebuilt. She offered to rent me a room for $50 a month. He made one more call and helped get me a job at a restaurant. With two phone calls, that priest changed my life and kept me from having to catch a return flight. His name was Father Sanchez, and I am forever grateful to him.

Our nature lies in movement; complete calm is death.
  – *Pascal*

Ultimately, the decision to step into the unknown was one of the best decisions of my life. I lived in the Caribbean for a total of six years over four separate trips and convinced many of my friends and family to move out there as well. It was there I discovered a passion for the ocean, spending my weekends on boats and exploring more than 60 Caribbean islands.

During that time, I had countless adventures. I got to fly a French fighter jet over the British Virgin Islands with a crazy ex-air show pilot. I went scuba diving on a 400-foot shipwreck at night during a full moon. I went hang gliding over a rainforest in Puerto Rico, and hiked the top of a volcano on Saba Island. I bought a timeshare on my own 38-foot sailboat off the coast of Puerto Rico and went sailing for days and weeks at a time.

Living in the Caribbean changed my beliefs about life and how society tells us we have to live it. In my travels, I have met people from all age ranges and backgrounds who decided to go see the world. Ninety percent of them did it without a lot of money. They just decided it was a must and figured out a way to do it.

I personally believe that long-term world travel is no harder than many things that you may have already accomplished in your life. With the following tools, nothing will stop you from seeing as much of this planet as you want. There is one thing every single one of us share, and that is a limited amount of time on this planet. There is such an incredible world awaiting you that nothing should stop you from seeing and experiencing as much as you want to.

If you take away only one thing from this entire book, make it this one:

The only thing that stops you from achieving any goal in life is a belief that you can't have it.

Belief is the Little Thing that Changes Everything

I once read that in some circuses, they take a baby elephant and attach it to a pole using only a thin string. After it grows to be an adult weighing as much as 14,000 pounds, the elephant will remain tied up only by the small thread. Nothing stops this elephant from breaking the string except a belief that it is not strong enough. One of the strongest animals on the planet can easily be held captive by nothing but a belief and a string.

All generalizations are false, including this one.
– Mark Twain

People are no different. For thousands of years people believed that it was impossible to run less than a four-minute mile. All the best athletes had tried it and failed. Scientists even said that it was not physically possible. One guy named Roger Bannister trained for two years and frequently did vision exercises where he imagined himself running less than a four-minute mile. Then he went out and did it. The funny thing is that within a decade, manyother people also broke the four-minute mile.

This is exactly how it is with beliefs about travel, except that travel is actually very easy. It is only our beliefs about travel that make it hard or expensive. Travel doesn't have to be either.

The only thing standing between you and absolute freedom is a piece of mental string.

Travel Killers: Why Some People Stay Home

What is amazing is that a belief is nothing but an idea that is conditioned to become a habitual way of thinking. One idea has the power to change your entire destiny if you believe it.

Fortunately, beliefs are not permanent. All of us change our beliefs constantly. There are times where we have a positive or negative belief about someone. We believe all sorts of ideas that are handed to us by our parents, our teachers and friends, television, books, society and so on. Most of us later change what we believe when we are exposed to new information that expands our viewpoints.

Beliefs are fine when they serve us, but when they don't; they can be one of the greatest sources of pain in our lives. The questions to ask are, "Have I chosen beliefs that bring me joy and happiness? Do I have a belief system that allows me to experience freedom and adventure and live in the magic of life every day?"

If traveling the world has always been a dream of yours but you have never actually done it, I guarantee that there is a belief that has been holding the door shut.

"Our beliefs are like unquestioned commands, telling us how things are, what's possible and what's impossible, what we can and cannot do. They shape every action, every thought, and every feeling that we experience. As a result, changing our belief systems is central to making any real and lasting change in our lives."
– Tony Robbins

TWO EMPTY REASONS WHY WE DON'T TRAVEL

Over a ten-year period I sold over $10 million worth of travel products through presentations that lasted from 30 minutes to several hours. I have literally talked to thousands of people about why they should make their travel dreams come true. The clients who were not traveling as much as they wanted always had the same excuses:

- I don't have enough time to travel.
- I can't afford it.

Expert traveler Travis Sherry at Extra Pack of Peanuts (www.extrapackofpeanuts.com) recently asked 71 major travel writers for a list of the reasons that people gave when asked why they weren't taking the trip they always wanted. I was blown away when I saw that they were the exact same reasons I had been hearing all these years.

- I do not have time.
- I can't afford it.

Some other common variations on the main two themes:

- They won't give me the time off (basically the same as #1).
- I have kids, and it's too hard to travel with them.
- I plan to do that kind of thing when I retire someday.
- I am too old to do something like that.

When you start to travel frequently and tell people about your adventures, you will be surprised at how often this is conversation comes up. Many people for some reason feel compelled to tell you why they would love to travel but they are just unable to do it. Some people feel threatened if they are not living up to their own dreams when they find out you are.

What is interesting is that each person says it like they are alone and special in having this challenge. Let me say this loud and clear. You are not alone – even a little bit. Every single person that manages to take a trip around the world or who travels frequently deals with or has dealt with the same challenges.

Some people may have had been financially successful, but if they did, it was probably even harder to get the time off. Or if they have lots of time off, they probably do not have lots of extra cash lying around. Both of these challenges are worth working around because what waits for you is the world and everything in it.

The jobs that pay the most often come with expectations to give up vacation time or work harder to justify such a high salary. At one point, I worked in a special department that only hired top salespeople. The company started to think that they owned us when it came to time off because they were paying people such large amounts of commissions. However, my brother and I always managed to get time off because we created value for our company and we decided it was non-negotiable. When we really needed time for something important to us and we were told no, we would let them know very non-confrontationally that we needed it in order to continue being employed. I realize that this sounds like a crazy idea, especially when the job market is tough for many people right now. However, in life you often get what you demand, and our gamble paid off every time.

---

*You will never find time for anything. If
you want time you must make it.*
– Charles Buxton

We would point out that if we could not spend time doing what we loved – which was travel – then simply making more money would not fix it. After all, what good is more money if you cannot translate it into the type of experiences you want to have in life? More money is simply more paper that you can buy things with.
Start buying amazing experiences through travel instead. Physical things can be lost, stolen or broken, but no matter what happens to you in life, you will always have those experiences.

I was stunned to learn two things: that Americans on average only get 11 vacation days each year (unlike workers in other first-world countries), and they generally use only half of that time. Being overworked and over-stressed is one of the major factors in heart disease, high blood pressure, anxiety, panic attacks, diabetes and cancer. The lack of relaxation and vacation time is literally killing people in large numbers.

This is your life, and it's ending one moment at a time.
— Chuck Palahniuk, **Fight Club**

So ask yourself, do I have more vacation time than I realize?

Could I negotiate more vacation time if I added more value to my work?

If I have the belief that I can do it, I shall surely acquire the capacity to do it even if I may not have it at the beginning.
— Ghandi

Another belief that is quite common for younger people is to plan on traveling when they get older. The problem is that old age comes with an entirely different set of challenges to overcome. Retirees are often on a fixed income, they have health problems or sometimes they are scared to travel overseas for the first time. Most older people would often tell me (if they were not traveling) is that travel is for younger people. I find this ironic. Young people think that travel is for the old people who (they think) have time and more money, while old people believe that travel is for the young who have youth and no responsibilities.

The truth is that you can find ways to travel at whatever age or financial position you are at in your life right now.

How do you begin? First start with a dream and then discover why you aren't living it.

How do you know you have found a travel goal big enough? When you see something in your mind that gives you a smile or a shiver of excitement, you are on the right track. You have found a dream worth pursuing, and if you hang onto that image and intensify it, you will be able to create it in your life.

God gave us the gift of life; it is up to us to give ourselves the gift of living well.
– Voltaire

I will ask you the same question that forever changed my life.

WHAT ARE THREE PLACES YOU WANT SEE IF YOU HAD SIX MONTHS LEFT TO LIVE?

Use this as an opportunity to brainstorm and come up with as many different ideas as you can. Every country you would like to see, everything you'd like to try – put it all down there. Dreams always come before resources. The vision always comes before the reality. What have you always wanted to do? Here are a few ideas to get you started.

Have you ever wanted to bungee jump or skydive? How about sailing a boat across an ocean? Have you ever wanted to take a river cruise through Europe or ride a camel next to the pyramids? What about listening to an opera in Tuscany or racing a Ferrari through the Italian Alps? Have you ever wanted to sit in silence and meditate in India for 10 days or watch a whale breach in Hawaii? Have you ever wanted to walk up and down the Great Wall of China or watch as a glacier shelf slides into the ocean in Alaska? Have you ever wanted to hang glide over a rainforest in Australia or swim with dolphins in Bali?

What crazy adventures or cultural experiences have always been on your list?

Imagine for a moment that you are experiencing your ultimate travel dream right now.

What would it feel like? What would you be seeing or smelling or tasting? Who would be with you? What would you be willing to do to experience this in your life?

If you still feel like you need more ideas, grab a copy of the book *1000 Places to See Before You Die* (www.1000places.com) and spend a few minutes reading it each day. Set up a journal to record the ideas that inspire you the most.

For those of the have the courage to live their dreams, life is one incredible adventure.

What are the top two things/beliefs that have stopped you from experiencing the travel dreams you just wrote down?

_____
_____
_____
_____
_____
_____
_____
_____
_____
_____
_____
_____
_____

The truth is that whatever belief (or story) you just wrote down has served a purpose. What purpose? These beliefs make us feel better about not going for what we really want right now. If we have a story about why we can't have something or why we will have it someday, we avoid some pain. Why? That story stops us from feeling like failures because we tell ourselves there's nothing we can do to change reality.

The truth is you can't fail if you never give up. As long as you are still making progress, you're still in the game. True failure is to never really try and to give up before you even get started.

two

Facing Fear, Smashing Excuses

The good news is that there is a very simple process to changing almost any belief. All beliefs are the mental equivalent of an idea that we stack evidence under until we have a feeling of certainty that it must be true. Some of them we are very certain about (for instance, that the sun will come up tomorrow) and some of them we are slightly certain about (our belief that Congress will agree on anything important). Virtually all beliefs can be changed and should be changed if they no longer serve our best interests. In order for us to change them, we really only need two elements.

The first is the acknowledgment that our belief will cause us pain if we do not change it. The second step is realizing that we will gain a lot more pleasure from a new belief because it will allow us to have what we really want.

So take a moment or two and look at whatever belief has stopped you from being able to travel and have experiences the way you want to. Then write out the two most painful things that having that belief will cause in your life. The more vividly you can describe these beliefs, the more effective this exercise will be.

Here is an example:

Old belief: "I do not have time to travel."

How will this belief cause me pain?

This belief will stop me from using the time I do have right now, and at the end of my life, I am going to look back and realize I never actually lived any of my dreams. I will end up spending all the time of my life working for other people and never for myself. I will lie on my deathbed and wonder why I sacrificed my dreams of fun and adventure so I could make someone else rich.

STEP 1

Name your old belief: Write it down in the simplest way possible.
_____
_____

Describe the pain you are going to experience if you do not choose a new belief:
_____
_____
_____
_____
_____
_____
_____
_____

There is very little pleasure or happiness in stories about why you cannot experience your dreams in life. Imagine the pleasure you will experience by living the dream you have created!

STEP 2

Once you have come up with some painful reasons about whatever beliefs held you back from your ultimate travel experiences, you can now take a look at the truth.

If you think you are too young to travel, then make your new beliefs, "Being young makes it easy to travel, because I can rough it a little to see the world by using youth hostels, campgrounds, couch surfing and flying coach." Or, "Right now is the best time to travel because I can actually enjoy it without worrying about my health."

If your old belief was, "I don't have the time," make the new one, "I have exactly as much time to live my dreams as I demand out of life." Or, "I have exactly the same amount of time as every other person on this planet." (This is true by the way. Time is the one thing that is equal for everyone.) Or, "I have as much time as I need if I use it wisely and create time for the things I really want to see and create in my life."

List your new beliefs here:
_____
_____
_____
_____

ARE YOU WILLING TO LOOK BACK ON YOUR LIFE SOMEDAY AND REALIZE THAT YOU MISSED YOUR CHANCE TO DO SOMETHING THAT IS THIS IMPORTANT TO YOU?

Most of us rarely ask ourselves these questions, but there are huge benefits in asking them now. Running out of time to see the world is one of the most powerful motivators you'll ever have. Every one of us will run out of minutes on this planet someday, but you do not have to leave a laundry list of unfinished dreams when you go.

Decide at this moment that you will not be one of those sorry souls who takes their dreams to the grave with them.

Let us endeavor so to live that when we come to die, even the undertaker will be sorry.
– Mark Twain

No Regrets

Bronnie Ware from www.bronnieware.com is a palliative care worker (someone who provides care for the last weeks of life) and wrote a book called *The Top Five Regrets of the Dying*. She discovered that the top two regrets people have in their last few weeks of life are these:

1. I wish I had the courage to live a life for myself instead of the life that other people expected of me.

2. I wish I hadn't worked so hard.

If the thought of lying on your deathbed and looking back at your life with massive regrets doesn't seem all that appealing, now is the time to start moving towards your dreams.

I recently found this short video about Zach Sobiech who was a great example for all of us of how to live fully in each moment. Zach was diagnosed with osteosarcoma (a rare form of bone cancer) at age 17 and discovered that he only had a few precious months to live. He chose to live completely with his friends, family and music and touched the lives of everyone around him up until May of 2013 when he finally succumbed to cancer. I highly recommend watching this video, which you can find by doing a Google search for Zach Sobiech.

My decision to move to the Caribbean changed every single part of my life. Since then I have traveled to 40 countries in addition to countless islands and had many amazing adventures along the way. I set a goal to see and photograph every country in the world before I die. I am amazed to live in a time where this goal is not only possible, but has already been done by many people.

One hundred years ago, I could not have a goal like this, even if I was the richest person on earth at the time.

Remember what Bilbo used to say: It's a dangerous business, going out your door. You step onto the road, and if you don't keep your feet, there's no knowing where you might be swept off to.
– J.R.R. Tolkien, The Hobbit

IF A BLIND KID CAN DO IT, WHY NOT YOU?

There are people with a fraction of our resources that are out there having grand adventures. Tony Giles is one great example. Tony is 100 percent blind, 80 percent deaf and had a kidney transplant in 2008. Most people would say that Tony was dealt a bad hand. Yet Tony has the heart of a lion. He has been to 81 countries, seven continents and all 50 American states. He's gone skydiving and bungee jumping 12 times (including once from 600 feet).

The most astonishing thing about Tony is that he has done most of his travel alone, with no travel partner. It still blows my mind that he somehow makes it all happen with these challenges. I often think of Tony when I feel like something is difficult or impossible and realize it is just a story I have told myself.

As you grow older, you'll find the only things you regret are the things you didn't do.
– Zachary Scott

CAN YOU IMAGINE LANDING IN A CITY LIKE BANGKOK BLIND, DEAF AND ALONE . . .

Tony did it, and now it's his favorite city in the world. If Tony can navigate the world without his sight, the rest of us can figure out how to take the time off or how to find the resources. Check out Tony's book *Seeing the World My Way* for a real-life example of all the adventures that are waiting for you.

During my interview with Tony, he told me that traveling the world taught him that his blindness is actually an advantage. He said that it helps people to see his true personality because they see him as less of a threat.

Tony created a belief system for himself that turns what most people would consider a handicap into an advantage. Thinking this way is what allows him to travel the world and have incredible adventures. If you ever think any travel dream is out of reach for you, picture Tony doing all those things alone and blind, and then go after your dream.

You can read more about Tony on his site www.tonythetraveller.com.

You can listen to my interview with Tony here: www.youtube.com/watch?v=UjIVntcL83A.

THE TRUTH: WHAT EPIC WORLD TRAVELERS BELIEVE, AND YOU DON'T (YET)

Back to Travis from Extra Pack of Peanuts, who did a great article about travel beliefs. He asked 71 of the most prolific travelers he could find about what they thought were the biggest beliefs that stop people from traveling and why they don't hold up. He got tons of great responses and gave me permission to use a few.

I need to give a bit of a disclaimer here. The next few paragraphs may offend a few people. I did a bit of soul searching and decided to leave this in even against the urging of my editor. There are definitely situations, which make travel almost impossible for some people due to a health, or financial crisis where other people are depending on them, etc. If that is you and you are easily offended, you can feel free to skip this section.

Every person I have met who has done something incredible has some fairly uncompromising beliefs in at least that area. They choose to change the world around them instead of changing their beliefs about what is possible. If I asked Arnold Schwarzenegger what his beliefs are about diet or working out, you will find them extreme compared to most people, which is why he gets extreme results.

That said, you do not have to adopt the belief system of these authors, but you will find one thing in common among them. They are all absolutely sold on the idea that travel anywhere in the world is completely possible. Because of this, not only have they been everywhere in the world, most have been traveling non-stop for one to five years straight. They could not do something like that without some seriously strong beliefs.

You can read the entire article here (www.extrapackofpeanuts.com/71-travel-experts/).

ROLF POTTS: AUTHOR OF VAGABONDING AND MARCO POLO DIDN'T GO THERE
www.vagabonding.net

The most common reason people give for why they can't undertake long-term journeys is that they don't have enough money to travel. This is a natural reaction in a society where money is seen as the solution to all of one's problems. The thing is, one only needs a modest amount of money (less, often, than one spends on day-to-day living at home) to travel the world for weeks or months or even years at a time. Money isn't our truest form of wealth in life; time is — and it doesn't take all that much money to allow oneself to spend one's time in a rich way.

Matt Kepnes: Author of How to Travel the World on Less than $50 a Day
www.nomadicmatt.com

Money. People think they need a lot of money to travel due to great marketing by travel companies, but as I and countless other people prove, you don't need a lot of money when you travel. Between discount cards, work programs, frequent flier miles, and sites like CouchSurfing.org, you can travel the world for pretty cheap if you really want to.

Benny Lewis: Creator of the multimedia course Speak from Day One
www.fluentin3months.com

Usually people will latch on to what seems like a totally logical reason to not travel, such as lack of money, no time, unable to get off work, family responsibilities and so on. At times these are legitimate, but many times the true reason they are not following this passion is fear, and the reason they give you when you ask is founded in nothing but this fear. They can repeat the mantra of "I have no money" all they like, ignoring stark evidence about how they should embrace minimalism and stop buying so much crap, or perhaps they think that learning a language is a rare genetic gift even though over half the population of the planet is multilingual. It's time they stepped outside of their self-fulfilling prophecies.

Lee Abbamonte: Youngest American to visit every county in the world (before age 30)
www.leeabbamonte.com

The two most common reasons people give me are money and time off. They are BS because if you have had any type of job in your life, you should have at least a little money saved and can work around the rest when you travel. You can travel cheaply, work your way around your travels and go from there. As far as time goes, make the time – if you have a job you can't get any time off, perhaps it's time to change jobs! Those are the two biggest reasons I get, and they are both BS. You don't have to be rich to travel, and sure, you need time, but you can make that happen if you really want to!

SEAN KEENER: CEO OF THE WWW.BOOTSNALL.COM TRAVEL NETWORK

The reasons I hear most often from folks about why they can't do independent travel are lack of time, lack of money, and other made-up barriers in the mind.

My answer after working with hundreds of thousands of travelers the past 15 years of why these reasons are not true is that they are truly myths. As humans, we have freedom of choice and everyday we make hundreds of decisions on how to think and what to do with our time. The reason folks don't travel is a choice that they make, not the reasons listed above. Go Indie Travel [independent traveling]. It's the best way to get an education (better than college and a better investment in yourself).

SEAN OGLE: FOUNDER OF LOCATION 180
www.seanogle.com

The most common response I hear for not traveling is, "I don't have the money." I'm sorry, it's not that you don't have the money, it's that you have other priorities – or perhaps have had a lifetime of other priorities and are now feeling the consequences. You can travel, but it might require some really uncomfortable changes. I had to sell my car and quit my job – but my desire to travel made it all worth it.

KATE MCCULLEY
www.adventurouskate.com

People often say that they don't have rich parents who will pay for them to backpack the world!

That couldn't be less true. Of all the people I met traveling the world, about 98% of them did so by saving money for a long time and using that money to travel. It's something that anyone can do, but not a lot of people actually do because they prioritize nights out with friends, or decorating their home, or buying lots of movies. If you prioritize travel and save your money, you can actually afford to do this!

Here are a few more responses some epic world travelers sent me.

Laurel Robbins
www.monkeysandmountains.com

I was just graduating from university and noticed that all my friends who had graduated a year before me were now "stuck." They had real jobs. Then came the car payments. Then came the condos. Then the furniture for the condo, and so the list went on. I wanted to travel before I became stuck as well. I had student loans so I did need to get a "real" job, which I found in the form of teaching English in South Korea, which paid quite well.

I became so addicted to expat life that I've now lived as an expat in four different countries and am currently residing in Germany when I plan to remain indefinitely. Travel doesn't always have to involve constantly being on the move. It can mean slowing down and settling into one place for a while, which I've discovered is my preferred travel style.

Johnny Ward
www.onestep4ward.com

Visited 100 countries before the age of 30. Social conformity, the media, our education systems dictate that we should go to school, go to university, go to a city, work in an office, save for a retirement then when we're old and frail, retire and enjoy the fruits of our labor. Personally, I don't want to do that. Not one bit. Saving for a retirement which may never come, or when it does come we're are too frail to truly enjoy it sounds like madness to me! Life is short – too short – and I want to enjoy mine every second of every day, so I try my best to do just that.

The more I travel, the more I realize that life was not supposed to be spent doing something you don't want to do. We're so lucky to have the opportunities we have. If I want to dive with great white sharks, I can do it; if I want to volunteer with refugees in Burma, I can do it; if I want to skydive over volcanoes in Indonesia, I can do it – and so can you, really (honestly, seriously!)! You don't have to be rich, win the lottery or rob a bank. You can live the life you want to right now, and not wait for the retirement that may never come.

Redesign your lifestyle, as I redesign mine and we can enjoy the ride together...

NANCY VOGEL
www.familyonbikes.org

It was, according to my husband and sons, a fairly simple wish: to ride bicycles from Alaska to Argentina. The trouble was that I was afraid – afraid that the mountain passes would be too high, the headwinds too strong. I was afraid the cold would be too cold and the heat too hot. But when I got really honest with myself, I realized my greatest fear was that I would fail. One night, as I lay in bed, I had one of those EUREKA moments! I realized that night that while I certainly had a good chance at failing if I tried, I also had a chance at succeeding. At the same time, if I never took that first pedal stroke – I faced a 100% chance of failure. When I looked at it from that perspective, it made no sense to not try. The rest, as they say, is history. Together as a family we spent nearly three years cycling 17,300 miles through fifteen countries. Against all odds, we made it.

FEDERICO SANDOVAL
www.maitravelsite.com

My need for travel started in 2001. I was reading a journal of somebody who owned her time, where she slept that night and where she would be the following day or weeks which is a freedom that very few people enjoy today. Many have in fact forgotten what real freedom is. The most common concern is money, followed by routine and stability. But if you think about it, when you own your and time you can set up your own routine and do what you want, when you want! If it's the future that concerns you, simply leave enough money to live with for a few months when you're back. You only live once, and if you search online or speak with others you will not hear of anybody that has regretted taking off to travel.

JODI ETTENBERG
www.legalnomads.com

After completing a two-year RTW, Jodi now lives a location-independent lifestyle and works from wherever she chooses. She wrote this after completing her first two-year journey.

A few weeks ago in Hpa-An, Myanmar (Burma), I was walking down Mount Zwegabin after sleeping on the floor of a monastery at the summit. It was just after dawn, and the claustrophobic heat of the day had yet to take hold. I was alone, and it was completely, almost eerily silent as I made my way to the valley below. Suddenly, I became overwhelmed – as in, tears pouring down my face overwhelmed – by how lucky I was to be there.

After so much saving and wanting and wishing, I was almost two years into a round-the-world trip and have never been happier. To say, "I want to save up money, quit my job and see the world – not to find myself, not to check off destinations from a list, but to soak it all up like a sponge," is one thing. To do all those things and then love every second of it (despite many ailments!) is a whole other realm of happy. Of all the wonderful consequences of my adventure, my uncontainable joy is the best of all. It has been extremely satisfying to have embarked on a voyage of this magnitude and to have been spot on about what I thought would drive me to continue traveling.

three

Craft a Compelling Travel Action Plan

The first step to catapult yourself towards your new travel dream is to create such a compelling vision that you'll be unwilling to let it go. To keep you motivated during the planning phase, your dream needs to start taking shape in the physical world. If your eyes, ears and mind see that your dream is real, everything becomes easy.

SEE IT AND BELIEVE IT

Almost nothing out there makes reaching your travel goals easier than having a clear mental picture of exactly what you're moving towards and having it in front of you daily.

Everything you have ever done in life has taken place in your mind first. This process happens so fast we hardly notice it. Even when we do something as simple as sitting down in a chair, we visualize it first. Sometimes it happens almost outside of our awareness, but it is still going on all the time.

Something as straightforward as creating a vision board can radically change the level of commitment and enthusiasm you have for a dream. By seeing your dream daily, you get an emotional impact. You brain looks at it and links the feeling you get from the seeing the image with your final goal.

Many people have used vision boards to create almost anything you can imagine in life, like relationships, wealth, houses, non-profits and gold medals, to name a few.

People have asked me, "Do I seriously need to cover my walls with photos of the places I want to go?" My answer is yes. Create a visual of something amazing on your wall, and you will find a way to go see it in real life.

The nice advantage about living in the media age is that you don't have to try to imagine things yourself. You can easily get an image online of virtually anything these days. This works with travel in particular because many of us will undertake a long journey in order to have a visual orgasm when we arrive.

The good news is that it doesn't have to be elegant in order for it to work. Many of the greatest achievers I have met have plastered sticky notes and photo cutouts all over their bathroom mirrors, car dashboards and bedroom walls. The only friend of mine who owns a Lamborghini carried a little photo of it with him for several months. He stayed so excited that he actually set new records at his company and made enough money to buy one.

Your vision board can also be massive. The first time I moved to the Caribbean, I was trying to get one of my friends Nick to move with me. In order for him to go, he had a huge list of things he had to do, like sort out a long-term relationship, remodel his house and sell it, and then quit a very good job.

The day I left, I took a poster of a perfect Caribbean beach and hung it on his wall. With a black marker I wrote on the bottom, "FIGHT FOR YOUR SERENITY." Six months later, he was sitting on a beach with me with a drink in his hand. He told me every day he would come home that winter dealing with snow and a relationship that was not making him happy and look at that poster. It kept him going when he was discouraged at the laundry list of obstacles he was facing, and he finally made it. Ten years later, he is still enjoying life on the ocean in the Virgin Islands.

If you have the urge to travel but you are not sure of the destinations that will inspire you the most, call a travel agency and request a stack of brochures. You can also check out photos of my travels at www.theendlessweekend.com or my buddy Trey Ratcliff from www.StuckinCustoms.com. His photos are amazing. Trey created one of the best jobs in the world for himself. He travels around the world taking amazing photos and teaching people how to do the same. He got so good at it that not only is he doing something he loves, and he is also very successful financially.

The most pathetic person in the world is someone who has sight, but no vision.
– Helen Keller

SEE IT AND CREATE IT

Dr. Maxwell Maltz wrote a book in the 1960s about the impact of visualization and identity called Psycho-Cybernetics. He did studies where they tracked the mental impact of people who had plastic surgery and found that people who visualized themselves differently changed the way they interacted with the world.

By seeing themselves as a different person, they acted differently and ended up with a different destiny.

Once they noticed this, they also studied people who had changed the way they look at themselves (through mental exercises) and found the same results. People and life in general will treat you the way you see yourself.

> *Imagination is a preview of life's coming attractions.*
> *– Albert Einstein*

Start seeing yourself as a person who travels widely and easily, who lives in an exotic location and who knows how to make things happen. As you look at your vision board, see yourself in that picture and imagine very specific activities you would do there. The more vivid and detailed your vision, the better.

SPEAK YOUR DREAM INTO REALITY

Any living thing needs food to stay alive, and the same is true for dreams.

A vision board feeds the very powerful visual side of you that knows that seeing is believing. But words have an amazing power as well. When you've decided to cut the excuses and put travel plans in motion, you may run into some doubts and fears that need to be tamed. Declarations tend to put those mental obstacles in their place.

What is a Declaration?

Basically it is a way to combine your goal with an action plan and repeat it to yourself daily. It's kind of like an affirmation but with much more emotional energy and intensity. Anything that we repeat to ourselves over and over with confidence becomes a powerful belief, positive or negative.

If you're half-hearted about your Declaration and are unwilling to invest any emotion into it, you won't get results. Plan to get yourself pumped first. Turn some music on that gets you fired up, and once you have a nice sense of confidence and enthusiasm; repeat your plan loudly and in the positive tense.

An even better way to do this is to go jogging. The physical exercise alone will put you into an amped up state of mind. Once you are there, you can easily condition your mind and create an intense state of faith.

Not sure this is true?

Think for a minute about how the US military can take someone who is a mild mannered person and turn him or her into someone willing to risk their life for their country. They can take someone who has a hard time following direction and make him or her follows orders without any hesitation. How exactly do they do this? They make people run miles and miles daily while repeating cadences. This is one of the strongest forms of mental conditioning there is, which is why it is so effective in assimilating someone into a completely new culture in only 4 to 6 weeks.

If you're planning a huge trip around the world, you could try something like the following cadence:

I am a world traveler. The money I needed came to me easily, because I choose experiences instead of more material junk. I achieved my goal of world travel because I was willing to do whatever it took to make it happen. Here are all the things I am committed to doing in order make this happen right now.

Then make a list of all the things you need to do to get your trip booked.

For instance:

1. Get time off
2. Get a cheap or free airline ticket
3. Find a place to stay
4. Research what you will be doing when you land

What cadence gives you that feeling of absolute certainty that you will get this done? Brainstorm here.

Once you have a few details in place, it's time to go public. Tell a few people (supportive ones) close to you that you have a dream, and you need their help to hold you accountable.

Remember that the bigger the dream, the more it's likely that some people will feel threatened by it and react negatively. When you succeed, it may remind them they failed to try. So choose the people you share your travel dream wisely. The wrong people may try to "protect you" by recommending something safer.

One of the reasons people stop learning is that they become less and less willing to risk failure.
– John W. Gardner

Luke Armstrong
www.theexpeditioner.com

Travel the world when you're young. When places like Egypt, France, South America and Australia are not just destinations, but limitless options. Travel the world because you can. Travel because most people can't or couldn't. Travel because you were born at a time in history when distance is merely a detail, an annoyance no larger than airplane meal portions. Travel while you still have time and freedom. Don't tell yourself you'll do it someday. Take out a calendar and make plans. Set a date and send me a postcard.

four

Clearing The Path:
Fear And The Time Vampires

Don't wait. The time will never be just right.
− N. Hill

CHOOSE YOUR FEAR WISELY

Fear can be your salvation in life or a death sentence depending on what you are afraid of. If you ask a world traveler what they are afraid of, they may say that they do not want to miss out on life. They may be afraid of running out of time before they actually experience as much as they want in the world. On the other hand, those who have never left their hometown may be more afraid of the unknown. People typically are most afraid of things outside of their comfort zone. As you expand your circle of things you've already done, it is much easier to try new things.

WHAT FEAR COULD PREVENT YOU FROM TRAVELING THE WORLD?

Make sure your fear is in the right place, and is motivating you to move forward and make your goal a reality. The more real your fear of missing out on your dream, the more action you will take, and the faster your dream will manifest.

I admit that I was afraid to quit my job and take a trip around the world. I had a career with the same company for 10 years and was making an extremely good income (double six figures). I moved forward because I finally decided that no amount of money could ever replace experiencing the world. I quit that job and despite their best efforts, I have never gone back. Why? Because having the freedom to travel and see the world is more important to me than having a nice car or nice house. I realized that with my travel savvy, I really do not need vast sums of money to travel. What I need is flexibility in my schedule so I can take advantage of all the opportunities I find so I can go see the world for little to no money.

When we do the thing we fear, death of fear is certain.
– Ralph Waldo Emerson

THE BLIND TRAVEL MASTER

There is no sure way to overcome your fear in life than to do the thing that triggers your fear. My friend Tony the blind traveler was completely terrified the first time he traveled by himself. He was going to school in South Carolina and decided to take a solo trip to New Orleans to overcome his fear. Once he got there and checked into the hotel, the first thing he did was to take a cab to the French Quarter. When he stepped out of the cab and was surrounded with the smells, sounds and energy of the French Quarter, he realized that he was alone. For a moment, he became terrified. His started to tremble and think about all the bad things that could happen to him. In that moment of panic, he decided to press forward anyway. He said that his trembling stopped, the fear instantly left him, and it has never returned like that again since.

The moment you act in the face of your fears is the moment they start to disappear and turn into excitement! The magic here is simple: make a small step toward your goal, and you'll have the courage to make another, and another.

If you're afraid about leaving your familiar, comfortable routine, plan a short weekend trip to get out of your rut and open your eyes to possibility. If you're not yet comfortable booking a plane ticket or hotel online, get a travel-savvy friend to show you how it's done. One small step will lead to another. What are the top two things/beliefs that have stopped you from experiencing the travel dreams you just wrote down?

_____
_____
_____
_____
_____
_____
_____
_____
_____
_____
_____
_____
_____

We are always getting ready to live but never living.
– Ralph Waldo Emerson

How to master your time and slay the time vampires

Once you have in place a goal and a vision, the only things that could slow you down are activities that suck away your energy and your time. In today's world, most people are surrounded by "time vampires" that make zero contribution to their real happiness.

What do I mean by time vampires?

We are bombarded with distractions. Television, Facebook, Twitter, computer games and texting keep us locked in front of screens instead of exploring our world. Surveys report that the average American spends 7 hours watching TV and 1.5 hours on Facebook – per day.

For those of you who don't have a calculator handy, that works out to 60 hours of screen time a week. Wasting 60 hours a week prevents you from making progress towards your dreams, and that's also 60 hours a week people are exposed to advertising.

That much advertising can robs us of our real dreams because it often convinces us that if we just had the right car, right house, right clothes or right gadgets that life would be perfect. Blowing time and money this way doesn't leave much for your dreams.

I am not judging, by the way. At the age of 27, I went through a period where I believed that success meant getting rich. I was working like crazy, I had my name on $2 million worth of real estate, a garage full of expensive cars and clothes, and I got caught in the trap of always wanting more. I am not saying that having nice things cannot be an important part of life, but Western society believes that the more you have, the happier you are, and it is 100 percent not true. If you always want more, no amount will ever be enough. And 90 percent of the time, experiences will make you more happy and fulfilled than material possessions ever will.

If I didn't define myself for myself, I would be crunched into other people's fantasies for me and eaten alive.
– Audre Lorde

> *Waste your money and you're only out of money, but waste your time and you've lost a part of your life.*
> *– Michael LeBoeuf*

Imagine what life would be like if you put that much time into pursuing your traveling dreams. For most people, killing their TV would allow them to achieve almost anything. One good solution is to cancel your cable and get Netflix. The $1500 you save a year can easily pay for a week or two of travel with the right travel hacking skills. You can still watch movies when you want to, and there are no commercials!

While backpacking in Europe, I met a teacher named Brian who was traveling for the summer. He worked in the evenings for a year as a bartender to save up the extra money. He essentially traded one year of Facebook and television for one of the peak experiences of his life.

Would you exchange some of your TV and Facebook time for a trip around the world?

Time vampires can also come in the form of people, unfortunately. Many of us have relationships that drain our time and energy. Have a buddy who's always nagging you to blow time and money at the bar? Or a friend who rants for hours about his or her latest drama?

Create exit phrases like, "Sorry, I have a bunch of stuff I need to work on," that let you out of a wasted evening. Decide not to pick up the phone every time it rings. Use a photo of your vision board as a screen saver on your phone and computer to focus your energy when you're tempted to throw it away. Invest in your own life.

Whatever dreams you choose, fight for them tooth and nail. Play it to the bone and choose your dreams over fear. Choose your dreams over other people's doubts. Choose your dream instead of watching other people lives on Facebook. Choose your dream and the whole world will help you.

We'll never be as young as we are tonight.
– Chuck Palahniuk

Life, if well lived, is long enough.
– Lucius Annaeus Seneca

When your life flashes before your eyes, make sure you've got plenty to watch.
– Unknown

five

Your Travel Dream Team

It's easy to think that living your dreams is a lonely business, but the truth is, if you're passionate about something – anything – someone else is, too. Surround yourself with voices that remind you that reaching your dreams is possible and completely within your power.

The world conspires to help those that are in love with the beauty of their dreams.
– Eleanor Roosevelt

It seems that our busy lives don't give us enough time to read, but Anthony Robbins turned me onto the idea of using NET time, which stands for No Extra Time. Anyone can listen to self-development courses, podcasts and audiobooks during your commute, while you're running at the gym, walking your dog, washing dishes or anything else where your brain is pretty much on autopilot.

In the last eight years, I spent roughly 3,000 hours doing various courses on CD and about 500 hours in person. I did it with the attitude that if I could just learn one thing that changed my life from each course, it will be worth the time. A few of them, as you can guess, were pretty horrible, but I also found a few amazing ones. The following are the ones that will make long-term travel (or basically any other goal) much easier.

Life-Changing Authors

The Four Hour Workweek by Timothy Ferriss

I had been planning on creating a travel and life coaching website for several years. When I saw Tim's blog, Experiments in Life Design, I was blown away because Tim had already created everything I envisioned and much more. Tim has lived and traveled all over the world and has several bestselling books. He is not only an epic world traveler and adventure seeker, but an ingenious online marketer. You can check out his blog by searching for 4 hour workweek.

Personal Power II: The Driving Force by Anthony Robbins

This course is about $300 brand new, but you can often find copies floating around on eBay for about $80. It has sold 40 million copies, making it the most successful course of its kind in history. A huge number of the most interesting and successful people in the world from Olympic athletes to U.S. presidents to CEOs have taken it. You listen to one CD each day for about 30 to 40 minutes and do a short exercise. This course had a huge, immediate impact on my life. After ten days, I felt like nothing could stop me from reaching my goals.

The Art of Non-Conformity by Chris Guillebeau

Chris is an unconventional guy who set a goal to see every country in the world in five years. He pulled this off in spurts of three to four months each year while running several companies, writing two bestselling books, doing two book tours and starting his own weeklong course for entrepreneurs called World Domination Summit. This gathering had 3,000 people attend its third annual event with another 8,000 people on the waiting list for tickets. His book is a must read for every aspiring world traveler. He also has a great blog where he offers travel hacking advice: www.chrisguillebeau.com/3x5/.

The Secret by Rhonda Byrne

Even though there is a bit of fluff to this movie, it does communicate a powerful message about gratitude and visualization. However, the creators should have emphasized that once you have your vision, you need to go out and take action to create it. The experts featured in the film speak from a fairly profound level of gratitude and certainly, that is quite contagious to watch. If you want to connect with a big dream, this is a fun way to do it.

Think and Grow Rich by Napoleon Hill

Even though *Think and Grow Rich* is not really a book about travel, it is a book about using your mind to achieve any desire in life. The same mental tools in this book could be used to do anything from finding your soul mate, traveling the world, build a business or taking a trip to the moon. This book has been a bestseller for almost a century for a reason.

A World in HDR by Trey Ratcliff

Trey's blog Stuck in Customs is hands down the best travel photography site on the Internet, and recently his photos surpassed 20 million views. Trey has brought high dynamic range (HDR) photography into the mainstream and inspired millions worldwide to travel with breathtaking images. His website is an excellent way to pick out extraordinary places to see, as well as learn HDR photography. In addition to a new post each day he also has some neat photography apps, tutorials and books.

When a person really desires something, the whole world conspires to help him attain it.
– Paulo Coelho

THE ALCHEMIST BY PAULO COELHO

This is a book has a simple story but multiple levels of meaning. Is extremely fun to read and has powerful messages about growth life travel and our real purpose on the planet. It is one of top five best-selling books in history.

1,000 PLACES TO SEE BEFORE YOU DIE BY PATRICIA SCHULTZ

If you do not already have a bucket list, simply pick up a copy of this book and get a highlighter ready. It is the ultimate list of amazing places to see and experience on the planet Earth.

> ...So many people live within unhappy circumstances and yet will not take the initiative to change their situation because they are conditioned to a life of security, conformity, and conservatism, all of which may appear to give one peace of mind, but in reality nothing is more damaging to the adventurous spirit within a man than a secure future. The very basic core of a man's living spirit is his passion for adventure. The joy of life comes from our encounters with new experiences, and hence there is no greater joy than to have an endlessly changing horizon, for each day, to have a new and different sun.
> – Chris McCandless

> You are the average of the 5 people you spend the most time with.
> – Jim Rohn

TRAVEL-HACKING EXPERTS

The easiest way to develop incredible beliefs about any topic is to hang around with people that already have those beliefs. Where can you find

50 to 100 incredible world travelers that will help you? Most of them are probably out traveling the world, but thanks to the Internet, they're very readily accessible on Facebook, Twitter and blogs.

A great way to change your life if you're going to be on social media is to go through and block or unfriend every person that puts negative information into your feed and then replace it with people that have the lifestyle that you want to have. Since I follow well over 100 world travelers on Facebook and Twitter, I am constantly getting photos, tips and inspirational stories whenever I open up those sites. You could say I consume a ninja traveler's social media diet.

By surrounding yourself with dedicated travelers, you get to ride their energy and borrow their expertise. Often the scariest, seemingly impossible adventures are just ones we have never tried. The easiest way to hurdle over fear of the unknown is to follow in the footsteps of people who have been there and done that.

I am including a few of my favorite experts and a quick description of their site (you may also want to check out the 12 that I mentioned a few pages back). When you see some of the incredible numbers of places or length of times some of these people have traveled, you would think they must be rich. As far as I know, not one single one of them is independently wealthy, and most of them have figured out how to make a living while traveling on a tiny budget.

Every man dies. Not every man really lives.
- William Wallace, Braveheart

WWW.BOOTSNALL.COM

This is probably the ultimate resource. Established in 1998, BootsnAll. com offers down-to-earth travel advice from many of the most epic world travelers. They post daily articles and advice that make doing a round the world trip easy.

WWW.EVERYTHING-EVERYWHERE.COM

Gary Ardnt retired in 2007, sold his house, started a blog and never looked back. He is the ultimate example of what travel should look like when you retire. In five years he has been to seven continents, 116 countries, 50 states, 125 U.S. national parks and 180 World Heritage sites. He isn't wealthy, so he traveled cheap and learned how to make money advertising on his website so he could keep going.

WWW.YTRAVELBLOG.COM

Caz and Craig Makepeace have been traveling the world since 1997 basically non-stop. On top of that when they had two kids, they didn't settle down, and they are still going. If you have ever said to yourself, "I will travel someday when my kids are grown," check out their site.

WWW.UNCORNEREDMARKET.COM

At the time that this book was published, authors Daniel Noll and Audrey Scott have been traveling for 2,225 days straight. They are photographers and storytellers and you will find lots of good advice on their site.

WWW.WILDJUNKET.COM

This is the blog of Alberto Molero and Nellie Huang who, since 2003, have slowly worked their way through over 50 countries. They spend up to several months at a time backpacking or stop and live in one spot for a while until the call of the road hits them again.

WWW.THEPLANETD.COM

Canada's adventure couple, Dave and Deb, share the craziest stories of attempting extreme adventures in some of the most remote parts of the planet. Some of their adventures include hiking Mount Everest, the Mongol rally and cycling across Africa. They're brutally honest about the ups downs and occasionally embarrassing moments of being a couple traveling long term.

WWW.BRENDANSADVENTURES.COM

I got a chance to interview Brendan who sold his first travel article online for $150, and with $500 in his pocket, decided to go see the world and write for a living to pay his way. It turned out to be harder than he initially thought, but he stuck it out, found his own blog and his own travel magazine Vagabundo at www.vagabundomagazine.com. He has been traveling non-stop for over two years now and with perseverance has built an impressive income stream, an audience and a list of insane adventures. Brendan also does a top 100 Indie travel blog list on his site if you would like even more travel info at your fingertips.

WWW.MOSTTRAVELEDPEOPLE.COM

This is one of the craziest sites I found while researching this book. It is a community where anyone can map out their travel conquest and see it visually on a globe. It is great for designing your world conquest. The site creators have gone beyond just a list of countries and broken the world up into almost 900 countries, islands and autonomous zones.

The world's super travel elite join have joined each other in a friendly competition to see who can wrap up all of them first. There are currently six or seven people who are quite close to finishing the entire list. They have also set up challenges and incentives to make things more interesting. The site's founders seem to realize that the travel ultimately is about the journey, not a competition, but they have still come up with a fun way for people to track their adventures and share them with each other.

Summary: Seven Concrete Steps to Put Your Travel Vision into Action

- Write down several things (or places) you want to experience.

- Whatever your goal, make sure you are really excited about it.

- Create a visual collage and flood your daily life with your vision. My original (round the world) photo collage took up almost an entire wall. Big dreams require a big vision.

- Envision yourself as an expert traveler. Every day, do something that connects you with that idea. Spend some time each day learning about the travel system, until you're expert enough to teach it to someone else.

- Sketch a plan and take action towards your dream now. Any small step brings you closer to your dream.

- Build faith in yourself by reviewing your past successes, repeating affirmations and taking in material (books, articles, audio books) that remind you that you're in command.

- Collect a dream team of travel experts. Connecting with a community of people that are already living the dream will keep yours alive. The more you learn from good people, the faster you will adopt the strategies and beliefs that work.

- Tell the world about your goal. You are even more likely to follow through after you tell your friends and family – at least the ones who will help you follow through. Neglect to tell the ones that will try to rain on your parade.

six

Wrangling The Details To Freedom

This section will help you quiet those voices that say it's all too hard. I'll give you my time-tested strategies for getting your life in order so you can easily move to another country or hit the road for a long trip.

UNTANGLING YOUR LIFE

At the end of the day, moving to a new country or city or taking a trip around the world is really just a laundry list of chores that need to be done. I have moved 11 times in 17 years, which means I move on average once every 18 months. I pretty much have this process down to a science, which makes it a lot less scary than when I packed up the first time. I realize that packing up is a big step for many people. Changing jobs and moving to a new city rank in the top five for most stressful life experiences. Why would moving to a new place make the lists of the top 5 of most stressful activities? People overwhelm themselves thinking about all the stuff they would need to do to move and the bundle of unknown components instead of focusing on what they are excited about and what they need to get done.

The secret to moving without the stress is not to leave everything to the last minute. Start two to three months in advance and chip away a little bit at a time. If you make baby steps each day, you will find it super easy.

So here a few tips for deconstructing your life so you can prepare for a long-term voyage or moving to a new city.

Step One

Shipping Secrets and Getting Rid of the Old Junk

These days, we acquire a fairly ridiculous amount of stuff we have no use for or rarely use. One of the best things about moving is getting the chance to start fresh and get rid of crap that has been weighing us down for years.

If you are moving out of the country or some place that you can not get to easily with a moving truck, the best place to start is by getting rid of anything you can't ship in boxes or take with you on a plane. You can often find a place to receive and store boxes for you until you get there by calling storage places in the area. Open an account for a small storage unit and start mailing them boxes. Then all you have to do is fly to the new destination, and once you find a new place to live, pick up your boxes and take them to your new house. This allows you to start the process of packing and moving in a few months!

I tend to maximize the luggage allowance for whatever airline I am flying with. Most airlines allow a checked bag that weighs up to 60 to 70 pounds and measures 60 total inches. Any local box store will sell boxes that are 20 x20x20 inches and if you pack it right you can get it just under the weight limit. You get two checked bags for free with some of the airlines, and often they are just $25 to $50 for each additional bag. I have seen my brother, who also moves a lot, walk into the airport with 10 to 12 boxes and pay about $500 in checked bag fees to move roughly 700 pounds worth of his stuff to a new city. I showed up to pick him up at the airport during one move, and he literally filled an entire SUV with boxes to the ceiling.

You will get a fairly comparable rate mailing boxes ground also. There is also an old trick for discounts on shipping if you use the USPS. Boxes of books have a highly discounted rate. So if you happen to have a couple of your boxes become "books," you will save a nice chunk of money on the shipping costs.

Whatever you cannot ship or take with you on the airplane needs to find a new home, somehow. If the move will be temporary – say under a year – then it may be worth storing some things or leaving them with family.

I've learned to unload my non-essential items in two steps.

1. Take everything that is worth selling and put it on eBay and anything too big to ship put on Craigslist. Craigslist is an online version of the classified section of a newspaper, except that you get to post ads for free.

2. Whatever you have left that is not going with you and is not worth selling, give away to friends or donate to Goodwill, Salvation Army. It really is that easy to get rid of a household worth of stuff. You will find you feel quite free and liberated as all of those things go out the door.

After moving so many times, I find the easiest way to transition into a new city or island in my case is to rent a condo for the first month so I can get a feel for the area and where I want to end up. You can find places like this on HomeAway.com or the other condo sites you will find in the accommodation section of this book. You can often rent a place for a month starting at $1000-1500 including utilities. This removes a lot of the fear of finding a place to live and gives you a smooth transition. You can take your time looking for the right place to live and not feel pressured into getting something right away while you watch hotel and food costs piling up by eating out all the time.

The last two to four weeks before you leave is crunch time. You will be doing lots of errands and to-do lists. You make sure you have paid all the final utility bills before you go and have your place cleaned. Give your notice at your work and go to the inevitable parties that friends and families will want to throw for you since you are leaving.

And that is really all there is to it. Moving to another country or breaking your life down to go on a long-term trip around the world really comes down to a bunch of BS chores. Get rid of whatever you cannot take with you, cancel all of your accounts and book a place to stay in the new destination. Once you land in the new city, just find a job and a new place to live. Moving accomplished, no problem.

If you need to keep the budget dirt cheap, you can also furnish the new place off of Craigslist also. You can always buy nicer stuff after you have been settled a few months. I have seen my brother furnish an entire floor of a house for $200 on Craigslist in about a week just by being able to pick things up from people when they needed them moved quickly. He had just taken a year off of work to travel and was trying to save money and you would have been amazed at how nice some of the stuff was that he got for free or quite cheap.

Breaking your life down to take a RTW is basically the same except you need to make sure you budget some money after your travel ends to reestablish a new place to live. In other words, set aside money for rent and a deposit on a new place so you have a smooth transition when you return.

Men talk of killing time, while time quietly kills them.
– Dion Boucicault

Untangle Your Life Recap

- Pick someplace awesome to live that you are super excited about.

- Do some research and get a idea what two to three months of expenses will look like – housing, food and transportation. Save up at least two to three months of expenses or more, depending on your comfort zone. Decide if you need a car in the new destination and what it will cost. You can always rent one for the first few months while you look for a good deal.

- Figure out the airfare cost to get yourself there or use the tools in this book to get a free ticket.

- Start the process of moving in advance by getting a storage unit in the new location and shipping boxes each week to the new location.

- Give away or sell anything that isn't going with you.

- Take care of any issues with the house your living in so you can leave.

- Get a monthly rental on www.homeaway.com or other house rental site.

- Sell any vehicles you own. If the move will be temporary, put them into storage with a storage place or family members.

- Cancel all utilities or bills you may have and make sure you give them an address for your final bill.

- Max out the carry-on limit and pay for a few extra bags or boxes if needed.

- Land in your new place.

- Find a new job and transportation.

- Call yourself a local and become the envy of you friends who still live in the same place they always have. If you just moved someplace tropical, go to the beach and drink copious amounts of rum. ☺

Part Two:

The Ultimate Travel Hacking Guide

Introduction

What exactly is travel hacking?

It is simply using creativity to make the resources you have go way further when traveling. It can apply to everything from backpacking to high-end travel.

One of my favorite travel hackers is Rick Ingersoll from the www.FrugalTravelGuy.com who earned in the neighborhood of 10,000,000 (yes, 10 million) frequent flyer miles by signing up for credit cards during promotions. Or a close friend of mine (who will remain anonymous) who got on a secret airline list that allowed him unlimited free flights for a year.

But travel hacking is more than scoring free ticket or place to stay. It's about making the whole trip go smoothly, from jet lag to great gear to finding the spots the locals love. I've collected information on the best websites, companies, gadgets and systems so you can save money, time and energy for living your travel adventures.

Like all things in life, I believe the ability to be a great travel hacker starts first with the dream and a belief that if I want it bad enough, there is a way to make it happen. Once you have your desire and your dream, almost anything is possible.

seven

Old-School Approach: Bartering For Travel

Many times all it takes in life to get what you want is simple to ask for it with a smile and an attitude of gratitude. A friend of mine, Brendan van Son, author of the blog Brendan's Adventures and the editor of Vagabundo Magazine, was staying at a youth hostel and managed to get an almost free trip on a cruise to Antarctica.

How did he do this?

He started a travel blog plus several social media pages to document his travels and offered to promote the cruise line on his website. This is not an uncommon thing to do these days. In fact, there are hundreds, if not thousands, of bloggers who trade publicity for travel. While he was there, he met another young backpacker who desperately wanted to go to Antarctica but who did not have the money to go.

Fortunately, he did have the right attitude. He walked down to the dock and managed to speak to the captain. He explained his situation and offered to work in the evenings cleaning, washing dishes or whatever was needed in exchange for free passage. The captain, seeing the young man's enthusiasm, could not turn him down and accepted his offer.

He did not get a lot of sleep during the 11-day cruise, but he did have the adventure of a lifetime for free and a better story than almost anyone else on the boat. The point is that travel hackers do not let things like a lack of money or resources stop them from going where they want.

They simply find another way, and most of the time, they manage to get where they want to go.

I had a similar experience for the tiny investment of a few minutes on the phone. I am a photographer, and I was looking for a place to stay for nine days on one of my favorite islands in the Caribbean called Virgin Gorda. I was shopping for villas online, and I noticed one that looked like it might be amazing, but the photos were so bad it was hard to tell. I Googled it and found a video that a former guest had made. I could clearly see it was beautiful. In fact, the place was for sale for $7 million and had six acres bordering the beach and a national park called The Baths. The Baths are five miles of boulders and caves surrounded by the most incredible beaches you will find anywhere.

I called the owner and explained that I could dramatically improve his photos and would be willing to do so in exchange for a week of accommodation on his estate. After about 15 minutes on the phone, he agreed and gave me three villas for the week. I took my whole family down and we had a blast. I helped a good friend of mine who designs websites do the same thing for his wedding. He exchanged a new website for having his wedding on another estate, also on Virgin Gorda.

This type of bartering can even work with big tour companies if you can connect with their marketing department. I got a $5,000 discount in exchange for photos from one of the larger tour companies in Europe last summer.

This kind of bartering for travel can be quite useful if you have something to offer. If you don't yet, you can always make it a goal to learn something worth trading. Some of the best options are photography, web design, SEO or teaching people to maximize their social media presence. You will find resources for how to learn and find these type of jobs in Chapter 18. Virtually every mom and pop resort and private villa owner needs help with these issues, so you might as well make a skill like these an easy ticket to free travel.

THE NEW APPROACH: HACKING THE AIRLINE POINTS SYSTEM!

Last year, I took a trip around the world which started out by taking a flight on British Airways from Washington D.C. to London with two flat bed seats in business class that take up the entire middle of the airplane. Yes, the seats were luxurious, but the best part was the price tag. I only had to pay for the taxes.

Forget waiting years to collect points or flight miles! I earned that many miles for signing up for just one credit card. My partner and I each got business class seats for 50,000 miles per person or 100,000 miles total. While I was on the phone booking the ticket, I went online and priced the ticket, and the normal cost was $8,400 for 2 passengers.

Imagine someone handing you $8,400 worth of travel for something that took five minutes worth of work. I was hooked at that moment, and a travel hacking junkie was born.

I also finally understood the big appeal of business class on long haul flights. It is a completely different world up in the front of the plane. We had the two seats in the middle of the plane right next to each other, and they both laid completely flat and horizontal into beds. Between the two of us, we had at least a king-size bed worth of space, complete with drawers for storage to personal entertainment systems and a three-course meal. I was having such an incredible time enjoying all the space and amenities that I actually forgot about going to sleep.

Enjoy yourself. It's later than you think.
  - Chinese Proverb

If this grabbed your attention, let's talk about how to do this for you.

Disclaimer:

First of all, I need to give a disclaimer that what I am not giving you advice on what decisions you should make with your own personal credit. I take no responsibility for any decisions you make. All I can do is tell you about my experience and the experience of many other people. Please use these resources to educate yourself so you can make your own decisions. In my experience, you most likely need a credit score of 680 or above to get approved for most of these offers. However, if your score is less than that, please read this section anyway. At the end I have included a highly secret method to boost your credit score by up to 100 points in as little as eight weeks.

The concept behind this type of travel hacking is signing up for secret "whale offers" from credit card companies. In a matter of 90 days, I earned more miles (about 750,000) doing this than I would have earned from 15 to 20 years worth of spending money and accumulating points the normal way.

I first learned of credit card churning from following Rick Ingersoll from the Frugal Travel Guy. There are many people who do this, but I believe he is the one of the best. Rick is a retired mortgage broker from Hilton Head who loves travel and started a blog so he could put his advice in one place for his friends and family. His advice was so good that over four years his website exploded and he ended up being interviewed by many of the big cable networks.

Everyone knows that credit cards often offer bonuses when you sign up for them. If you have pretty good credit, you probably get them in your mailbox all the time. Most people, however, are unaware that the best offers are not sent out in the mail and can only be found with links to the offers. I included exactly where to find these secret offers later on in this chapter.

One huge credit myth is that if you sign up for more than one new credit card every few years, your credit score will tank. While it can lower your score slightly when you create a new inquiry, it is usually an insignificant amount and it is also temporary.

So far, Rick has opened up 90 credit cards in about 9 years and still has a credit score of almost 800. Every two years, inquiries fall off. So a smart travel hacker will monitor and maximize this process so they can sign up for bonuses as much a possible. Rick normally watches what offers are out there, and when he submits an application, he does three or four on the same day so that none of them are visible to his other applications. This also means that inquiries made on the same day fall off on the same day as well.

You can also have a lot more credit lines open at one time then you might think. Matt from www.nomadicmatt.com had 31 one cards open at once last time I talked to him and his credit score was still great. The reason it doesn't hurt you is that it actually improves your debt-to-income ratio as long as you're not leaving balances on the cards.

eight
How to Get Unlimited Free Airline Tickets

THE MILLION-MILE CHECKLIST

1. CHECK YOUR CREDIT SCORE

Your credit score needs to be at least above 650 FICO to play this game, and ideally it should be between 680–720 and above. You can personally pull as many scores as you want without affecting it at all. Why? It is different than a financial institution doing it because when you check your own score, you are not applying for credit. You have the right to see your own info.

If you have a low credit rating, see page 64 for a nearly instant boost you can use.

Follow these websites to find the best "whale offers" as soon as they come out.

- www.TheFrugalTravelGuy.com
- www.Flyertalk.com
- www.extrapackofpeanuts.com

All of them will let you know when the secret deals are and which cards are worth it. A good rule of thumb is that any card offering over 50,000 miles (if you can handle the minimum spend and there are no crazy yearly fees) is a sweet deal. Those 50,000 miles are worth about two domestic coach flights or one international flight on average. Try to sign up for three or four on the same day if possible, and wait 90 days before signing up for more.

How do you know if the minimum spending requirement is okay? It is based on your cash flow that you will spend on during that same period anyway. For instance, if the minimum to spend to get the bonus is $1500 in 90 days and you're going to be spending that kind of money on some kind of a credit card or debit card anyway, then you should be safe.

2. Organize your new hobby

Set all cards up on an automatic payment system so you can never miss a payment. I recommend setting them to pay the balance in full and then only spend money you would spend anyway. This will make sure that you never spend money unnecessarily or pay interest for no reason. If this is not an option, at least set them to pay the minimum payment so you can never be late.

3. Sign up for Award Wallet
www.awardwallet.com

Award Wallet is awesome for two reasons: It's free, and extremely easy to use. The concept is pretty simple. Enter your user name and password for every frequent flyer mile or other loyalty account you have. On one screen, Award Wallet keeps updated records of how many miles or points you have in each one and also stores all of your user names or frequent flyer numbers for each account as well. The best part is that you can log on to all your accounts from one home screen. For example, instead of having to enter your user name and password to log on to British Airways, you just click on your BA account and it instantly loads the website and logs on for you. One the reasons people with miles in several programs don't use them is the amount of time that it takes to go from one airline's website to the next. Using Award Traveler and Award Wallet makes it extremely easy not only to find flights, but to book them quickly.

If you want to also organize the rest of your accounts in one place, you can also use a service like QuickBooks. This makes it simple to monitor your balances on your different accounts. While you're at it, you can organize the rest of your financial life at the same time, since the program also tracks bank accounts, investment accounts and other financial balances.

Keeping your new hobby simple: A complete system for churning credit cards

My ongoing goal is to sign up for and earn large bonuses on as many cards as I can, and do it in a way that makes it easy to keep track of everything.

- One of the tricks to keeping a stable score when you are opening and closing credit card accounts is simply to leave two or three of your oldest cards (four years or older) open even if you're not using them much. This helps show a longer credit history and helps stabilize your score. Closing an account that you have only had open for a short time like one or two years often will make very little difference.

- You can sign up for a credit card monitoring service such as TransUnion for about $14 a month. By signing up for a service like, this you can watch your score and make sure it stays in the range you want it to. If you open up too many accounts and your score drops too much, just give it some time for your new accounts to age until your score recovers. It is not an exact science, but a rule of thumb for is that a new card lowers my score by about three to five points at most. This usually is just for the first three to six months however, and then it recovers.

- The minute I receive a new card, I put it onto an auto pay so there is no way I can ever be make a mistake and be late on a payment.

- The other way to easily organize many cards at once is QuickBooks. You can enter the user name and password for each account and see all of your account balances on one page, making it easy to keep track of them. You will log onto one page and it will update the balances and information for all of your credit cards at one time, saving you the hassle of logging into multiple websites.

- Most of the time, the cards will have minimum spending requirements within the first 90 days to six months. It is important to make sure that you would be spending this amount of money during this time period anyway and simply use the card to pay for everything until you hit the amount. On most of the cards I received, the spending requirement was $1500 in 90 days; on another it was $5000 in 6 months. I simply used one at a time until I got my bonus, and then I was on to the next one.

Amazon Payments www.payments.amazon.com

The other trick to hitting the spend requirement is to send a family member $1000 a month with Amazon Payments and then have them send it back to you. You simply use any frequent flyer miles credit card to make the payment just like PayPal. Since you are using the card to make the payment and it looks just like a purchase at Amazon, you get miles for the transaction. Amazon lets you send the first $1000 for free unlike PayPal, which would charge you 3 percent. This is a easy way to earn an extra $12,000 miles a year for each of you, while hitting the minimum spend requirements faster on new cards you sign up for.

Wallaby Financial www.walla.by Wallaby Financial figured out a way to give you just one credit card to carry that is linked to the rest of your credit card accounts. Most miles cards may offer two to five times as many miles for spending money at certain retailers. For instance, one card may give you double miles for gas, another one for restaurants or office supplies and another for airfare. When you have several cards to manage, it can become tough to keep track of which card is better for which location.

This card from Wallaby Financial will allow you to use one master card (like a master key) and then route the charge to the credit card you have that will give you the most points for that given situation. So if one card gives you extra points for gas, it will put the charge on that one if you are using it at a gas station. The idea has some limitations, but I could see it being quite useful for racking up lots of extra points without having to be as organized about it.

Hacking airfare: Why a huge stack of miles beats a stack of cash

People sometimes ask me if this is a lot of work. Not at all! It's a game you can play to win flights all over the world for free. Most people who actually have the money to fly wherever they want to often don't actually do it because they'd prefer to spend their money elsewhere. With frequent flyer miles, there is nothing else you can spend them on but travel.

On my first round of credit card signup (in one day), I opened five cards and banked 350,000 frequent flyer miles. That many miles are equivalent to seven round-trip tickets airline tickets to Europe or up to 14 domestic flights.

In my case, I turned the points I got from those cards into the following:

- Two business class tickets from Washington, D.C. to London
- One coach ticket from Miami to Costa Rica
- One coach ticket from San Juan to Costa Rica
- One ticket to Hartford, Connecticut
- One ticket to New Orleans
- Two coach tickets from Washington, D.C. to the Caribbean.

The best part about having a huge stack of miles and points to use is that there is no guilt about spending miles on an airline ticket – not even a business class or first class seat. Even if you have plenty of money in the bank, you can always find something else to spend it on, like bills, the kids' college fund etc., but with a nice stack of miles in the bank, you have no other option but to use them on travel, and it feels so good to spend them!

When was the last time someone gave you 14 free airline tickets for one hour of work on a computer?

The Gangster Approach: Try pushing a bank around for a change!

Once you have already signed for a few of these cards, it can be fun to make them earn your business once in a while. Most credit cards have a special department whose job is to keep you from cancelling by giving you miles or waiving your yearly fee, if you have one. All you have to do is call and ask if there is a department you should talk to if you want to cancel your credit card. Most of them will say yes and transfer you right away.

I made one of these calls once while on a treadmill at the gym.

Here is how it went:

Operator: Hi, sir. I understand you want to cancel? May I ask why?

Me: I have way too many credit cards, and I want to sign up for a new one that is giving away a ton of free miles. I don't want too many open at once, so I want to close this one.

Operator: I see you have been a valued customer since 2008. We would really like to keep you. If you would like to keep this card open I can give you 5,000 miles and they can be in your account in the next 30 days.

Me: Is that all you can do?

Operator: Or I could give you 5 miles for every dollar you spend up to 15,000 total and refund the annual fee from last year!

Me: That should work. Sign me up!

All I did was then use that card only for the next four or five weeks, and wham! I ended up with enough miles for a free one-way domestic ticket.

You also gain lots of flexibility when flying with miles since you can change your dates on most airlines without any major penalties. This gives you the freedom when you are enjoying yourself to just call the airline and stay for a few more days or a week on a whim.

Seasoned Trade Lines: The secret trick to boosting your credit score

What if I have no credit history or my credit is not quite good enough?

I accidentally learned a very secret (but legal) trick to improve your credit score called seasoned trade lines. Normally, the only way to improve your credit history is to get new accounts and then wait several years for the history to be long enough to actually matter. What I learned is that if you have a spouse or family member with great credit (or even close friend), they can actually add you to a couple of their cards and instantly hand you years worth of their credit history. There are actually companies that charge you to do this, but if you have someone who wants to help, there is no reason to pay for it.

There are two ways you can add someone to an existing credit card. The first way is by adding them as an authorized user. This shows up on their report, but in my experience, it did not make that much of a difference in their score. The second way is to add them as a co-applicant. Even if they have horrible credit, most banks don't care because they still have the main account holder on the hook. The difference is when you get added as a co-applicant, it gets reported to your credit history as if you have had the account since the day it was originally opened.

If you have bad credit or not a lot of credit history you can instantly gain five or even ten years of good credit history in a matter of weeks. One of my close friends raised his score a hundred points in two weeks this way and was able to buy my house because of it.

Recap:

If your credit score is not enough to get approved for these cards or anything else you want to buy, have yourself added as a co-applicant to a friend or family member's credit cards. The older the card and larger the credit line, the more it will boost your score. It helps more if the cards they add you too do not have a balance on them. The co-applicant never has to have a physical card. They just have to be added to the account.

Jumping through some of these hoops may seem like a shell game, but if you have always dreamed of seeing the world, then it is one of the best games to learn, ever! As Rick Ingersoll of the Frugal Travel Guy said during our interview, he still can't believe how easy this is. Not only has the recession not stopped the flood of free miles coming from these offers, they have actually increased the amounts. Since people with decent credit scores are even more of a commodity these days, the banks have ended up spending huge sums of money to get new customers or steal them from other banks.

nine
Making Airlines Work for You: The Stack-Your-Miles Strategy

It's really worth spending a bit of time on Wikipedia learning about the three airline alliances. Get to know them so you can better maximize both earning and spending your miles on flights.

Here is a very quick overview:

- Star Alliance has 27 member airlines with 21,100 daily flights.
- SkyTeam has 19 Member airlines with 15,500 daily flights.
- Oneworld Alliance has 11 member airlines with 9300 daily flights.

Star Alliance is the clearly the largest and has great for flights from the U.S. to Canada, Europe, Asia and most parts of the Middle East.

You can have miles with one alliance airline and use them to book flights on their partners. For instance, I take miles from United and use them to book flights on United, Lufthansa, Swiss Air, Austrian Air and U.S. Airways, among others. This may sound complex, but the reason I use United is that their website makes it super easy to find flights, they have good availability and they are priced really well.

START STACKING MILES USING AIRLINE ALLIANCES!

1. Sign up for United, American and Air France frequent flyer (FF) miles accounts. There are several other good programs out

there, but these three have some major advantages (especially for beginners).

I chose these three programs because each offers the best FF program for their particular alliance of airlines. An airline alliance is a group of connected airlines that agree to book passengers on the same flight and share other resources (see page 69 for more information).

By having one account in each major alliance, it allows you to earn miles almost every time you fly a major airline. Instead of having a small stack of miles spread across accounts with every airline out there, you can have all your miles funneled into the three best programs so they stack up faster and you get free tickets.

- United covers all the airlines in Star Alliance
- American covers Oneworld
- Air France covers SkyTeam

2. Anytime you fly any major airline, look up which alliance it is under and give them the appropriate mileage number for one of the three FF accounts. As an example, if you are flying Air Canada, you would give them the United Airlines FF number since both airlines are in Star Alliance. Even though you're flying a Canadian airline, the miles you earn will be deposited in your United mileage account.

Why should you stack miles in these three programs?

1. Low mileage redemptions for coach and business class flights.

2. Easy-to-use websites with good search engines.

3. Good availability for FF mileage tickets on their own flights.

4. Wide open availability for award travel for their alliance partners. This one is super important. If you have good partner award availability, FF miles are good with 20 to 30 airlines instead of just one.

5. All of them allow you to book a one-way ticket for half of the miles (some airlines charge you full price for a one way or 66 percent of the cost of a round trip).

6. Both United Airlines and American Airlines have very low taxes (normally $50-$150) on a ticket. In contrast, many of the European airlines have taxes as much $400-$800 a flight.

7. Air France still has fairly high taxes, but they still are the best option in SkyTeam and they still have great availability and an easy to use website. They are also a 4-star airline, which offers both good seats and service.

The key with all of this is that you do not need to actually fly these airlines in order to take advantage of their programs. There are 28 airlines in Star Alliance, and I can find seats on most of them on the United Airlines website to book with my UA miles.

I can also fly all of those 28 airlines and earn UA miles with them. Since you could do this same with any of the 28 airlines in Star Alliance, it makes sense to pick the one (UA) that offers all of the advantages above in terms of ease of use and overall value of the program. The same thing applies for both American Airlines and Air France. If you're new to mileage programs, these three are the best place to start and focus your stack of miles you earn flying.

As you sign up for credit cards, you will end up with additional FF accounts simply because you need to have one in order to receive the big stack of miles you get as a bonus. This is no big deal, however. When you paying money for a ticket in any of the three alliances however, use these three FF numbers as your default so that you can maximize the miles you earn by concentrating them into the same three accounts instead of spreading them out among many.

SPECIAL REPORT: EXPERT ADVICE ON AIRLINE ALLIANCES

Here are links to information on each alliance plus my tips on working with them. Each page details which airlines are included as well as where their hubs are located and the main routes they fly.

STAR ALLIANCE
www.en.wikipedia.org/wiki/Star_Alliance

Snapshot: The best value for your miles in terms of awards for Star Alliance will be Air Canada, United. These airlines are by far the best, not because you are going always going to fly with them, but because it is easy to book flights with them, they are priced well and it is pretty easy to use their miles on many other airlines. All Nippon Airways also has some big advantages because they have more liberal rules about stopovers and round-the-world tickets. Most airlines make you return the same direction you came, meaning that if I fly from the U.S. to Europe, I am not allowed to come back through Asia. ANA does not have this problem, making it easy to book RTW tickets with them.

With ANA you have to calculate the actual ticketed mileage for each flight to find out the number of miles. They often work out to be a better deal than the other carriers, however, it not as easy to use their program when you are just starting.

ONEWORLD
www.en.wikipedia.org/wiki/Oneworld

Snapshot: Oneworld is the second best alliance to store miles with.

American and British Airways are two of the best awards programs in Oneworld. American's website is pretty user friendly and flight availability is decent and well priced if you book them in advance. If you wait until the last minute, they will charge double or triple the amount of miles for the same flight. British Airways has great planes and service and lots of nonstop flight to Europe as well as partners with service to Asia. You have to be careful when you fly with them to any airport in London however, because the taxes can be quite expensive even if you are just stopping for a layover.

SkyTeam
www.en.wikipedia.org/wiki/SkyTeam

Snapshot: If I have a choice when flying, SkyTeam is my least favorite. There are times you will end you flying them anyway, so you might as well earn miles.

For SkyTeam, your best bet is Air France. Their main hub is Charles DeGaulle Airport in Paris, and they offer great non-stop flights from the east or west coast to Europe. Delta can have some good flights, but you often need more advanced software to find their flights. I've often found them to be very difficult to deal with.

Special Report

Never Wait on Hold Again: Top secret airline phone numbers!

Many airlines have special phone numbers they give out to elite travelers. I am including a few of them for the major airlines' award travel departments to make it easy for you to book a reward flight. I have had no problem calling them even if I did not have any special status with the airline. You normally should have little to no hold time when calling these special departments.

American Airlines Elite: Gold - 1-800-848-4653

Delta Gold number - 1-800-325-1551

Air France (SkyMiles) - 1-800-375-8723

United Premier Exec - 800-325-0046

British Airways ExecClub - 800-452-1201

US AIR - 800-428-4322

Air New Zealand - 800-262-1234

Air Canada Super Elite - 800-401-7201

Men for the sake of getting a living forget to live.
– Margaret Fuller

ten

The Ultimate Endless Weekend: Buying Your First Round-The world Airline Ticket

The first website I stumbled upon that showed me the dream of traveling long term was www.bootsnall.com. I was in awe of how many places you could add onto one ticket for such a low price. Imagine buying one ticket for around $3,000 that allowed you to fly to 25 countries!

Most airline tickets, for whatever reason, have rules that say if you go halfway around the world, your return flight must come back the same way.

If you continue on until you make it all the way around by going the same direction, then it becomes different type of ticket (meaning a different set of rules) called a round-the-world ticket or RTW. Most airline tickets also have rules limiting the number of stopovers, which is a layover of more than 24 hours. Most tickets will allow a stopover and they will also allow an open-jaw ticket, which means you fly into one city and return home from another one.

If you try to get more exotic than that, the prices can start to skyrocket when buying traditional tickets.

RTW tickets are bulk or discounted tickets usually within the same airline alliance that are not limited by either the number of stopovers or the direction of your flights. This allows you to add many flights without paying more for that privilege. Normally, it is up to 16 destinations inside of one ticket. On top of that, many of the airlines will discount their portion of the total flight at very low rates as long as it is part of an RTW. That doesn't necessarily mean that the airlines are discount airlines, though. In fact, when I took my trip last year, I flew part of it on one of the only six airlines in the world rated five stars (Kingfisher) and had quite a few four-star airlines also. Most airlines are rated 3 stars or below, so a 4 or 5-star airline is basically as good as it gets.

The rules for a round-the-world ticket are pretty simple. You can spend as much time as you want in any destination as long as the entire trip is no more than one year. And for many of them, you have to keep moving forward direction around the world. You can't retrace your steps or have multiple stops in the same destination.

What's amazing is at times you can buy $20,000 to $30,000 worth of airfare for as little as $3,000 to $6,000. There are companies that will help you find the best routes, like AirTreks in San Francisco. AirTreks is a full-service travel agency that does nothing but book round-the-world tickets. Their software, which is quite simple, helps you create your itinerary. If you need travel ideas, they normally have anywhere between 15 to 20 pre-planned routes you can use as a starting point. Their itineraries are fully customizable.

Here are a few examples (taken from spring 2013 prices):

AROUND THE WORLD BY AIR AND LAND

This is a crazy trip for people who have decided they must travel to every continent in less than a year. You can easily add 10 to 15 more countries to this itinerary (or any other one that stops in Europe) for the same price by just paying a Eurail pass or taking an independent travel tour or a group tour through Europe when you stop.

Around the World by Air and by Foot

From $5,060 to $5,735
includes taxes of $765

Los Angeles – Guatemala City – San Jose (Costa Rica) – Quito – Sao Paulo – Johannesburg – Nairobi – Cairo – Athens – Istanbul – Dubai – Kathmandu –Colombo – Kuala Lumpur –Bali (Denpasar) – Perth – Sydney Christchurch –Auckland – Rarotonga (Cook Islands) – Los Angeles

Amazing Adventure

From $ 4,345 to $4,975
includes taxes of $1,150

Los Angeles – London – Nairobi - Kilimanjaro – Zanzibar – Dar Es Salaam – Johannesburg – Cape Town – Dubai – Singapore – Kuala Lumpur – Chiang Mai – Bangkok – Phuket – Singapore – Brisbane – Sydney – Nadi (Fiji) – Los Angeles

Circle Atlantic

From $1,829 to $2,339
includes taxes of $350

New York – Bogota – Rio de Janeiro – Paris – Madrid – New York

Best of South America

From $2,275 to $2,575
includes taxes of $575
Miami – Quito – Lima – Cusco – La Paz – Santiago – Puerto Montt – Punta Arenas – El Calafate – Buenos Aires – Miami

BIG GAP YEAR

From $3,984 to $5,184
includes taxes of $985

San Francisco – Hong Kong – Hanoi – Saigon / Ho Chi Minh City – Bangkok –Phuket – Bali (Denpasar) – Singapore – Kuala Lumpur – Delhi – Bombay / Mumbai – Dubai – Addis Ababa – Nairobi – Johannesburg – Cairo – Istanbul –London – Reykjavik – New York – San Francisco

This should give you a basic idea of what a RTW ticket and what it can do for you. It is not needed for every type of trip, but can often be perfect anytime you want to do something more creative than just your basic round-trip flight to the same city. To teach you how to put together a round-the-world ticket I put together a short tutorial (6 minutes) that walks you through the process. You can also easily add a Eurail pass and knock out 10-20 countries in Europe with just one stop there. You simply give yourself several months and ride the trains around or take cheap intra-country flights.

LINKS AND RESOURCES FOR BUYING A ROUND-THE-WORLD AIRLINE TICKET:

- Here is a link to my free video tutorial: www.theendlessweekend.com/buying-the-ride-of-your-life-a-tutorial-on-round-the-world-airline-tickets.

- I also highly recommend reading www.bootsnall.com

They are a huge resource center for anything to do with RTW travel and you will find tons of good articles on all kinds of subjects to help you plan a RTW trip.

They actually just recently launched a website called www.indie.bootsnall.com that allows you to price and instantly book your own multicounty airline ticket yourself right on there website. This is the first time you can actually book a ticket with more than six stops without a travel agent helping you.

- Here is a link to the specials page for AirTreks where you will find lots of great starting points for your round-the-world trip. www.airtreks.com/airfare/specials

- Here is a link to an article by Matt from Nomadic Matt or RTW tickets. www.nomadicmatt.com/travel-tips/buying-a-rtw-ticket

---

Our battered suitcases were piled on the sidewalk again; we had longer ways to go. But no matter, the road is life.
 - Jack Kerouac

How to book flights like a travel agent by using ITA Matrix

The best people in the world at finding great deals on flights, aside from travel agents, are airfare brokers. I recently got a job working as an airfare broker because I knew it would be a good way to master the global travel system. I have always done pretty well as finding good deals on airfare, but the skill set of some of the brokers that I met is unsurpassed in the airfare industry. This is how I learned about Matrix. Google runs it, and no one other than travel agents has ever heard of it because you cannot actually book an airline ticket with it.

It is wired directly into the backend of most of the airlines' computer systems, and it can find flights better than anything else I have found. Once you find the flight, you can call any travel agent or the airline directly and give them the flight information. Then they can book the flight for you with no middleman.

Here is a quick example: My brother asked me to help him find a flight for his girlfriend. The flight went like this: New York–Rio de Janeiro-New York City-Maui. They had been looking at website like Expedia, and the best price they had found for was $3,476. I did a search for the itinerary as a multi-city flight and found a package with very short layovers on Delta for $1,231. All they had to do was spend 20 minutes on the phone with Delta and give the flight numbers, and they saved $2245. Not a bad return for 20 minutes of work.

Here is how to use this software like a pro:

First go to http://matrix.itasoftware.com/search.htm.

You can also Google Matrix ITA.

1. Select your destination and dates like you would in any airfare search engine.

2. Choose the flexibility you have for destinations and dates. ITA gives you the following options: the day before, the day after plus or minus one day plus or minus two days. You get to choose these options for both your outgoing and return flight individually, which gives you quite a bit of flexibility.

3. Select the class of service you are looking for – cheapest available, business or first class.

4. Once you have your search results, you can filter by the departure or arrival times. If you click on the drop-down tab that says either arrival or departure, you can select a specific time range or select multiple time ranges that you're looking for (for example, 5 p.m. to 9 p.m.).

5. Once you find the flight, simply call the airline and give them the information. They can book it for you over the phone. In spite of the step of making a phone call, you will find that this

is the fastest, most accurate site out there and gives you better pricing than anywhere else.

It is better to travel well than to arrive.
– attributed to the Buddha

GET A GURU: FINDING DISCOUNTED FIRST AND BUSINESS CLASS

I highly recommend amassing your own stack of credit card points and miles so you can fly free. However, if you are going to pay for a ticket in the front of the plane, you might as well get it for a huge discount. International business flights normally run between $4,000 to $6,000 for flights (from the U.S.) to Europe and Asia and $8,000-$11,000 from the U.S. to Australia. Why on earth would anyone pay that kind of money when they could fly coach for $700 to $1,500? One big reason is a seat that turns into a bed so you can sleep all the way there. There are lots of other perks like better service and food, but the bed is really the main thing that anyone cares about.

An airfare broker is able to find or create flights that are impossible to find any other way. By create, I mean that they take advanced software, and using groups of airlines within an alliance, create a flight that the airline's own software does not create for whatever reason.

There are about five companies that do this, and they were able find me flights between $3,000 to $3,500 to Europe and Asia and $4,500 to $5,500 for Australia. I am not going to recommend one since my opinion may be biased,
but Google search discount business class and you will find about five companies that specialize in this.

These companies assign you a personal agent who looks at your flight using every possible angle and approach and finally comes up with the best flight for the money. Their fee for finding the flight for you is included in the price.

SPECIAL REPORT: BOOKING THE BEST SEATS AND AIRLINES

Not all airlines are created equal. The best way to find out if you are about to book a two-star carrier with horrible seats and service is to research it first.

Star Trax: http://www.theendlessweekend.com/5_star_airline

This site will help you know exactly what to expect before you book your flight. They give you the star rating for the airline as well as for the class of service you are about to book. You can also read reviews by passengers and see what flight and equipment they were flying. The rule of thumb is that all U.S. airlines are 3 stars and most European and Asian carriers are 4 stars out of 5.

HOW CAN YOU MAKE SURE THAT YOU GET A BUSINESS CLASS SEAT WORTH FOR PAYING FOR?

Most international business class flights offer seats that flatten out completely. However, some of them recline to between 55 to 65 degrees, which means that the seat itself is flat, but it is still at a slight angle. This is a vast improvement over coach seating, but the very best ones actually recline 180 degrees flat like a bed.

Unfortunately, there are still some bad airlines out there that still offer the older cradle-style seat (which is essentially a coach seat with leather), and they charge the same money for that.

The easiest way to tell before you pay big bucks or spend your points for business class is to check a website called www.seatguru.com or www.

flatseats.com. You enter your airline and flight number and see a layout of the plane, seats and full details of what kind of aircraft they are flying before you book it. This is also a good way to find out type of planes and seats are the best when booking a coach flight also.

Without new experiences, something inside of us sleeps. The sleeper must awaken.
– Frank Herbert

---

eleven

A Simple Guide to Amazing Accommodations: How to book mind-blowing places all over the world for the lowest price!

If you have taken a look at the section on airfare, you should already have some pretty good ideas on how to get to your next country or even trip around the world for a the lowest price possible.

That brings us to the second half of our equation: finding perfect, and affordable lodging anywhere in the world.

I look at lodging in eight different categories:

1. Staying in hotels seems obvious, of course, but knowing how to use the right tools and resources to find the best deals can make a huge difference in whether you have to break the bank to stay someplace nice. People are frequently amazed at how easy it is to stay at 3-, 4- and occasionally even 5-star hotels for less than what they're paying for horrible hotels.

2. Renting houses apartments and flats is probably the most cost-effective and overall best experience if you're traveling for more than a week. You can often get a place for a month with a kitchen for less money than you'll pay for a decent hotel for one week.

3. Staying in youth hostels can easily quadruple your savings on housing costs, but there are some huge differences between a good youth hostel and a bad one.

4. Couch surfing may seem like something just for the adventurous because you're essentially staying as a guest in somebody's home, but in another way, it's actually great for the faint of heart because when you show up in a new country, you have somebody local to show you around. The other nice benefit to it also that it is typically free.

5. An expert travel duo wrote a book on their experience house sitting all over the world for 500 days straight. They didn't pay for a single hotel or single accommodation anywhere. You may have to feed somebody's cat, but for a free villa or house, it really is not a bad trade-off.

6. House swapping is quite similar to house sitting except you trade houses with somebody. This is quite popular, and there are literally tens of thousands of places listed. This works even better if you happen to have a house in a popular vacation spot. If you happen to live someplace that nobody wants to go, it may still work, but may not be as convenient.

7. Timeshares are a good option because there are over 7,000 time-share resorts in the world. There are ways to get access to timeshare inventory without actually buying a timeshare, and some of them are quite incredible because they offer full kitchens and lots of great amenities.

8. Camping may not be your cup of tea in your home country, but can seem a lot more exotic when it is someplace on the other side of the globe. Some of my favorite places to camp include the British Virgin Islands and deserted beaches in Costa Rica. Costa Rica was free and the British Virgin Islands site was $25 a night.

> *"Yesterday is gone. Tomorrow has not yet come. We have only today. Let us begin."*
> – Mother Theresa

Deals & Steals:
Finding the best possible price on a hotel

For me personally, the best place to shop for hotels and often airfare is hands down www.kayak.com. Why is it the best place? Pretty simple. It is an easy-to-use interface that allows you to search about five different websites at the same time.

Here are a few of the key points.

- When searching from the home screen on KAYAK for hotels, always click the "select all websites" button at the bottom so that it will search all websites at the same time. This, unfortunately, will launch about five browser windows, but it's completely worth it because different websites will have different prices and this always shows you the best price for whichever hotel you're looking at. There can be a difference of as much as a $200 a night between one website and another for the same hotel.

- Once you have a general search result, use the main kayak browser window that aggregates all them (not the windows that launched for all the other websites). On the left-hand side you'll notice that that you can deselect certain star ratings of hotels. For instance, if you only want to see four-star or better hotels, you can deselect all other hotels. This is extremely useful if you don't want to wade through all the bad hotels.

- Once you've done this, you can sort results by price from low to high. This will instantly show you the cheapest 4- or 5-star hotel available. If there's nothing in your price range for 4 or 5 stars, you can always reselect 3 stars and simply filter again.

- Another extremely useful thing about KAYAK is that you can also search for hotels within a certain distance of an address or point of interest like a convention center, monument or an airport. You'll find the two tools to do this on the left-hand sidebar. Once you type in the address, you can then select the maximum distance that you would like to be away from that address.

It also quite useful to take a look at the map view of hotels if you're familiar with a city or the points of interest in the city. Once you are in map view, you can still click on the individual hotels on the left sidebar.

There is a peculiar pleasure in riding out into the unknown. A pleasure which no second journey on the same trail ever affords.
- Edith Durham

Renting Condos, Apartments and Vacation Homes

There are several companies that specialize in residential lodging, but by far the one that I have the best experience with his www.homeaway.com. They not only been the cheapest but also offered some the nicest places, the best photos and more detailed descriptions and the easiest search functions.

Here are some quick search tips:

1. Enter your destination, dates and how many bedrooms you want.

2. Filter the results based on prices from low to high.

3. Scroll through the 2 to 3 pages of results and look at all the ones that are in your price range as well as just above your price range. Pick out your top five to ten choices and put together a 3- or 4- sentence email something similar to the following:

I am interested in renting your place from December 10th –January 10th. I will take really good care of it. Is there any way you could take $700 for the month instead of $1,000?

Send a lowball offer to each of the five to ten places you really like. It only takes a few minutes and you will get three or four takers out of the group. This is how you end up staying in a really nice condo that feels like home instead of being crammed into a small hotel room.

In fact, while I was on their website doing research for this chapter recently, I just found a ridiculously cheap 1-bedroom apartment in Buenos Aires for only $350 a week, (that's before asking for a discount). It has hardwood floors, a high-end kitchen and furnishings and comes with access to a rooftop pool. (Take advantage of the kitchen while you are there and you can eliminate two of the top three expenses to travel.) If I go with free with miles, my entire trip will cost me about $400 more than if I stayed home. Even if I eat out a few times while I'm there, it still does not really raise my daily living expenses.

Another good site, which also has a mobile app, is www.airbnb.com. They have lots of apartments and flats around the world ranging from budget to luxury accommodations. In addition to finding a place to stay, you can also rent out your own place while you are gone, if you would like. They currently have 150,000 places listed in 190 countries.

One of my friends, Scott Dinsmore from www.liveyourlegend.net, recently went to Thailand. Not only did he fly for free in business class using signup bonus points, but he rented his San Francisco apartment on Airbnb for $2800 while he was gone. Since living expenses in Thailand are pretty cheap, he covered the cost of his hotel, a couple hours of massage and most of his spending money. He said he trip cost him pretty close to zero dollars after the rental income.

YOUTH HOSTELS

The issues to consider with hostels are the amenities, the clientele and your expectations. Some places will be a little more family oriented, while many will cater to younger backpacking crowd. I've stayed in some very nice ones in as well as a few that were very annoying because loud guests made it hard to sleep.

Accommodations can range from anything from a room full of bunk beds to private rooms. In a situation where there are people sharing a room, there will be separate shower areas as well as lockers so your valuables will be safe. Even if the bedrooms are basic, many hostels will have lots of other amenities built into them, from nice restaurants, lounges, pool tables and even swimming pools and nightclubs!

The main advantage to hostel stays is rates, which start at about $15 and increase to around $35 per night. Hostels also make it extremely easy to meet people, so if you are worried about traveling on your own, stay a week at a youth hostel and you will quickly have more friends than you know what to do with. You end up meeting people from all over the world – most of them single.

Here is a great article meeting members of the opposite sex while traveling. www.theendlessweekend.com/haven_for_singles

The most important thing about staying in a youth hostel is getting the right one. How do you find a good one?

Fortunately, there is a website that's very similar to KAYAK but dedicated to youth hostels, campgrounds and inexpensive hotels called Hostel World. You can find it here: www.hostelworld.com.

1. Input your travel dates as well as the place you would like to visit; they will list all of your options for you.

2. Go through the photos and information about the hostel. More importantly, read the reviews so you know exactly what to expect and pick the one with the right energy level for your trip. Oftentimes, each place has an average of 600 to 700 reviews, so it is quite easy to know exactly what to expect when you and what they will offer for accommodations, amenities etc.

Man cannot discover new oceans unless he has the courage to lose sight of the shore.
– Andre Gide

COUCHSURFING INTERNATIONAL

"Couchsurfing saved me lots of money and gave me more authentic experiences than I ever could have gotten without it. Having lodging (and a lot of times some portion of my food) covered made it so the last real cost hurdle was transportation. Once I started hitchhiking, even that was somewhat alleviated. If you're open, adventurous, and trusting, you can travel cheaply and immersively."
Roni Wiess: http://roniweiss.com

Couchsurfing has several different options. It is a network and community of roughly 65,000 people all over the world who volunteer to host travelers or least assist in some way (it wasn't created by surfers or hobos). It provides a way for people to have a much more authentic travel experience and those trying to maximize the distance they can go for the same money.

To use Couchsurfing, create a profile and meet other people that are part of the network. When traveling to a different country, you can meet people who have an extra room that will lend it out to travelers. On other occasions, people may just give you advice or play tour guide for you for the day. It will all depend on the level of relationship that you build with them. As long as people feel comfortable with you, they are very likely to offer use of their extra room. You can rate your host and vice versa so future Couchsurfer guests and hosts know what to expect.

If it makes you feel more comfortable, another way to get involved is to host travelers. You can offer an overnight spot for people who are coming to your area, especially if you live someplace people like to visit. One of my good friends Cody did this for a one-year period, during which time he had eight or nine people stay with him for roughly for a week. He enjoyed playing tour guide and now he has five or six people who want him to come visit all over the world. Next time he goes to Europe, he automatically has a few places to stay and friends to show him around

To get an in-depth view of what couch surfing is like check out the movie One Couch at a Time. It is the real story of veteran Couchsurfer Alexandra Liss through 21 countries, 6 subcontinents, for seven months using CouchSurfing.org.

You can watch the movie online for $5 here: www.onecouchatatime.com.
Here is the website: www.couchsurfing.org.

HOUSE SWAPPING

Live it up in mansions for free by swapping your house!

Had enough of paying for hotels? Wish you had something nice to stay in that felt like home?

If you are just a little bit adventurous, house swapping may be the way to get you out there. The concept is pretty simple. You sign up for a membership to a website (the 2 largest ones are www.homeexchange.com and www.homefor exchange.com) and swap your house with someone. The neat thing is that there are some incredible houses on there. HomeExchange has 42,000 listings in over 148 countries. This means you can pretty much go anywhere. Depending on your preferences, you may be able to swap cars as well and cut out the cost of a rental.

There are tons of people who use this as the primary way to travel. One thing I found interesting is that there is a site dedicated just to teachers because teachers and other professionals tend to trust each other. And teachers also are one of the few professions that actually get three months off every year. Unfortunately, since most of them are not paid extremely well even though they may have the time, they may not have the money to travel for extended periods during the summer.

The good news is that using the house swapping as a resource along with free airline tickets from frequent flyer miles can make living abroad for the summer just as cheap as staying home for any teacher.

If you take advantage of one of the many ways to fly for free or cheaply, you can easily use these sites to travel for the same cost as staying home. Many of the people I have spoken with who travel this way do so for two to eight weeks at a time. This is the kind of travel that is out of reach for most people and a completely different type of experience than staying in a hotel room. You have access to a kitchen, for starters, which saves you a fortune on food during your stay and a house that is fully equipped with whatever you need.

Nervous about having someone in your place while you are gone?

You can always remove a few items that may be personal or too valuable to leave lying around and put them into a storage unit or a friend's house for the week or month. Paying $100 for storage is a small cost for your own flat in the French Quarter of Paris or your own ski villa in Aspen.

Make sure you check your car and home insurance to see that they will cover your guest. Most companies will, but you should check anyway.

HOUSE SITTING

The nice thing about house sitting is that normally the people who are concerned enough to bring in a house sitter have some pretty nice places. One of my friends recently house sat for four weeks for a doctor in San Francisco and lived in a place worth several million dollars for free. All she had to do was feed the cat while she was there. To get a more in-depth training on house sitting you can read *How to Become a Housesitter and Travel the World* by Dalene and Peter Heck. They traveled for three years straight and spent over 500 days house sitting. In their book they review all of the big house sitting websites, teach you how to make an effective house sitting profile and offer tips on getting good reviews as guests. Here is the link: www.hecktictravels.com/housesitting.

You can also check out this article by Nomadic Matt on house sitting: www.nomadicmatt.com/travel-blogs/house-sitting/.

Here are a few house sitting and house swapping websites sites:
- Home Exchange – www.homeexchange.com
- HomeForExchange – www.homeforexchange.com
- HomeLink International – http://home-exchange-usa.com
- Exchangeaway – www.exchangeaway.com
- Global Home Exchange – www.4homex.com

House sitting sites
- www.luxuryhousesitting.com/about.php
- www.housecarers.com
- www.mindmyhouse.com

TIMESHARE RENTALS

Timeshare rentals give you the same advantages that you would get from either house or condo rentals. The main difference is that resorts often will have even better amenities than hotels do. These features may include water parks, game rooms, golf courses, beach activities, and more. They will often host activities and tours from the resort as well. Something to look out for though is that sometimes they may offer you freebies to entice you to do some type of tour of their resort (sales pitch). My advice is to resist the freebies because you will most certainly earn them with the amount of time you spend with a salesperson. If they say the tour will be 60 to 90 minutes, you can probably expect a 2- to 3- hour presentation, which eats away your vacation time.

1. When renting a timeshare the key is to do quite a bit of homework on the resort and even the section of the resort you will be staying in. The best place to find reviews is www.tripadvisor.com.

2. If you're staying with the major brands such as Wyndham, Disney, Marriott, Hyatt, Hilton or Westgate, they should be very luxurious and have lots of amenities.

3. two best websites to find timeshare rentals are www.ebay.com (search for timeshare rentals) and www.redweek.com.

CAMPING

My version of camping typically entails hanging up a portable hammock up on the beach or a waterfall somewhere and sleeping until the next morning. If the hammock idea sounds like your cup of tea, check out www.hammockbliss.com,
which offers deluxe hammocks. You can buy a portable hammock in a bag that you can throw into a backpack complete with hanging ropes and mosquito netting. There are few things more peaceful in life than swinging in a hammock next to the ocean on a tropical island somewhere. It is also pretty nice in a park or just about anywhere else you can find a couple of nice trees.

If more adventurous camping is your ideal way to see the world, I'd definitely recommend these sites:

1. www.hostelworld.com is a search engine for campsites all over the world.

2. www.parksandcampgrounds.com is useful for searching for campgrounds inside the United States.

I am not the same having seen the moon shine on the other side of the world.
— Mary Anne Radmacher

---

twelve
Amazing Tour Companies And Travel Discount Websites

One of the ultimate goals of world travel is to be getting to the point where you can freely move throughout the world without needing to take tours and use guides. We've all had that visual of a "traditional" tour company with tourists in Hawaiian T-shirts clicking away on their cameras, never leaving their hotel except for when they're with their group.

While some of the best experiences to be had while traveling will be found a little off the beaten path, there are lots of really good tour companies out there that are interested in supporting the local community and helping you experience their culture. If you are new to international travel, it can be a good idea to start off with a few tours, if they're a good match for your dreams and pace. There are also some places you really cannot visit without one, like Tibet or Machu Picchu. The big upside to a tour company is that a good one will take you to incredible places. The downside is if the tour is one with a tight schedule, you may end up feeling rushed or herded like livestock.

Adventure Tours

National Geographic
adventure.nationalgeographic.com/adventure/outfitterhome

If you have ever wanted to do try adventurous travel like hiking to the top of Mount Everest or Kilimanjaro or even hiking the mountains of Patagonia or Peru, going with an adventure tour company may be the right way to get your feet wet. They can show you the trails and bring the equipment for you for your basic beginner hiking, and for the more extreme mountaineering, they can help you reach the top and come back alive.

The best place to find adventure tours is on National Geographic magazine's website. The NG editors reviewed the main players in the tour business a while back and built an interface that aggregates around 200 of them. Unfortunately, the interface on the website is a little bit cumbersome, but they do have incredible information.

What is great is that you can search and filter through tour companies by price point, continent, user reviews or the type of adventure you're looking for, such as hiking, mountain climbing, safaris, volunteerism travel, winter sports, etc.

Incredible Adventures
www.incredible-adventures.com

Did you ever have a fantasy of flying with a fighter pilot at 2,000 miles per hour to the edge of space with one of the best pilots on earth? If so, it's probably a lot more attainable than you realize. In Russia, they let you pay for rides in military fighter jets like the MiG-25. Prices start at about $2,500 and go up to $10,000.
They literally take you to the edge of space where you can see the curve of the earth and blackness above you for $10,000. They also can arrange things like whale or shark encounters, jumping out of hot air balloons or HALO (high altitude low opening) jumps, submarine adventures and much more. Basically this company can make a man's

James Bond fantasies (at least the ones not involving women) come true.

A man of ordinary talent will always be ordinary, whether he travels or not; but a man of superior talent (which I cannot deny myself to be without being impious) will go to pieces if he remains forever in the same place.
– Wolfgang Amadeus Mozart

TRADITIONAL TOUR COMPANIES

WWW.AFFORDABLETOURS.COM
Another good search engine for more traditional tour companies. You can search by price range, dates or country. They also have independent travel tours if you don't want to be with a big group.

WWW.GATEONETRAVEL.COM
I first learned about Gate 1 Travel on my first trip to Costa Rica with a friend who was a travel agent for American Express. She was widely traveled and had already been to around 40 countries by the time I met her. We used them book to a really cool tour around Costa Rica for five days. Gate 1 Travel offers both independent and escorted tours. They give you the option of land-only pricing or airfare-included pricing. They also have packages that range from 3- up to 5-star hotels. A seven-day tour land package with them typically ranges between $600-$1200, including accommodations.

A journey of a thousand miles begins with a cash advance.
–Alton Brown

Discounted Tour Companies

Pavlus Travel
www.cheapertravel.com

If you're looking for more discounted travel, this site has tours ranging from hostel and indie travel all the way up to more traditional tours.

Contiki
www.contiki.com

This tour company does a great job of showing you a million places in a short period of time on a tiny budget, but I would not recommend them unless you are under the age of 28 and also enjoy mixing your travel with heavy drinking. If that is your preference, then they do an incredible job. You will see many places for not a lot of money, but be prepared for a party that goes late. Think frat house party and you will not be far off.

Travelzoo
www.travelzoo.com

Travelzoo is another interesting discounter; kind of like the Groupon of travel websites. They have a list of their top 20 deals at any moment, and I've often seen three- to four-day packages with airfare and hotel for roughly $300-$500. The catch is that you normally have to go on very specific dates. This can still be fun if you have a flexible travel schedule or are interested in last-minute specials.

Luxury Tours

Abercrombie & Kent
www.abercrombiekent.com

If you are at the point in your life where you are interested in luxury adventure travel it probably doesn't get any better than Abercrombie & Kent. National Geographic rates them the number one luxury tour company in the world. They specialize in things like luxury safaris, and a 12-day tour with them will set you back $4,500- $7,600.

TAUCK
http://www.tauck.com/

This company specializes in luxury tours and European River cruises. They mainly cater to an older crowd and like to surprise their clients with high end amenities.

One of the saddest lines in the world is, "Oh come now - be realistic." The best parts of this world were not fashioned by those who were realistic. They were fashioned by those who dared to look hard at their wishes and gave them horses to ride.
— Richard Nelson Bolles

---

thirteen

Cutting Edge Travel Gear

After spending four months of research, I put together some of the neatest gadgets and websites I discovered for long-term travel. If you want to save yourself a ton of research and money, check out these companies first.

Eagle Creek suitcase: Many backpackers recommend traveling as light as possible and recommend just a backpack. Some of them almost treat getting by with minimal luggage as a spiritual challenge.

Rolf Potts, the author of Vagabonding, actually made it around the entire world once with just a carry-on backpack. Traveling that light isn't really an option for me as a photographer, since I carry my camera gear as my carry-on bag.

My main goal was to move my camera gear and other electronics all in my carry-on and everything else in one checked bag. I chose a rolling bag instead of a backpack, because when walking long distances, having easily rolling, well-balanced suitcase is a lot easier on the back than a backpack.

This type of setup has worked out really well for me. I am still highly mobile with the Eagle Creek checked bag and carry-on, and I am much better prepared than the average traveler. Since the wheels carry the load I have zero strain on my back. I have seen lots of backpackers walking with 70 pounds of stuff strapped to their backs and front and they are actually a lot less mobile than I am.

I looked at almost every possible rolling bag before finding Eagle Creek. I believe that this is the best luggage system in the world, period. The suitcases come in many different sizes, but I decided on the Tarmac 25 inch. Eagle Creek makes these things to take a beating. They are lightweight and have highly reinforced corners. The wheels are huge, indestructible and will roll over anything from dirt to cobblestone. The handle is sturdy, comfortable and has no flex to it. You can watch a video review here: www.youtube.com/watch?v=LNIymB_P4ik.

After taking this suitcase over 100,000 miles in 24 months, it still barely has a scratch on it. It's been tossed into planes, thrown into boats, taken over cobblestone streets, dragged through sand and nothing has made a dent. I have actually been hoping I can find a way to break it because it has a seven-year warranty, so if it breaks, then I get a free replacement.

Pack-It: Eagle Creek also created a unique packing system called Pack-It that keeps your stuff organized. It compartmentalizes your clothing and other items into sections. It allows you to keep your clean and dirty clothes separated and fit two to three times the amount of gear in the same space. Each Pack-It container shrinks the air out of your clothes and keeps thing looking pressed (relatively speaking). You can watch the video here: www.youtube.com/watch?v=DODw1Yeb_04&feature=related.

Pacsafe: This is backpacking equivalent of a mobile safe for your backpack or suitcase. If you ever need to leave a camera or computer in your hotel room (or hostel without lockers), this gives you peace of mind. It expands and creates a wire mesh that allows you to lock your backpack to an object in the room and keeps someone from taking it or even going through it. I would only use this when leaving your luggage in a room; if you put it on all the time, it will probably just make your bag look more like a target. It is useful in a situation where you feel want to feel more comfortable leaving your stuff in your room, especially if you have electronics. http://pacsafe.com/pacsafe-85l-backpack-protector

Belkin Adapter: This is the smallest and lightest travel charger I could find. It will charge three normal devices plus two Apple devices (iPod, iPad, iPhone) at one time. http://www.google.com/shopping/product/10976838794359756869?hl=en

Nokia mobile phone with an international SIM card: There are several good companies that offer international SIM cards. A quick Google search will give you lots of options to choose from. I chose a company called World Sim (www.worldsim.com) because it gave me a U.S.- and Europe-based phone number with super low rates. In most European countries, outgoing calls are 20-35 cents a minute. Incoming calls are 20 cents a minute if they called my U.S. phone number and free if they called my European number. There may be certain countries (especially in Asia or anyplace remote) where it is worth getting a card specific to just that one country.

Virtual Post Mail: These guys are amazing. For $10 a month, (the first three months, then $20 per month after that) they receive and scan your mail for you so you can read it online. They also store packages for you until you get home and then mail them to you. For $5, they deposit any checks you receive in the mail with your bank, so you get access to your money right away.

I have to say took advantage of these guys just a little bit. I asked them what their limit was in the amount of packages I could have them hold for me, and they said they didn't have a limit. So I then proceeded to mail them packages from almost every other country that I went to. Once I got home after traveling for six months, it only cost me about $400 to have all the packages mailed to my new address. www.virtualpostmail.com

Mail A Letter: If you are excited by the idea of never opening your mail again and wish you could complete the cycle and never have to mail anything, check out www.mailaletter.com. You can send a physical letter on this website starting at $1.52. Simply type the letter and pay, and they print it and mail it for you. http://www.mailaletter.com/

International credit card: Almost every credit card company I checked charges 3% every time you use your card outside the U.S.A. except for the Chase British Airways, the United Explorer and the Chase Sapphire Preferred cards. You also can earn 50,000 to 100,000 miles for signing up, which will get you a round-trip ticket to Europe for free (you just pay the taxes).

PackTowl Ultralight: A super absorbent towel that takes up virtually no space. It isn't exactly a beach towel, but it will work fine if you stay in a hostel that doesn't offer them. www.rei.com/product/830600/packtowl-ultralite-towel

WorldMed Travel Insurance: If you are going to be traveling for several months, it may be worth buying worldwide health insurance. For $342, I insured two of us with a 4-month policy that covered up to $500,000 for medical expenses. It also includes insurance for trip interruption, emergency evacuation, passport replacement and concierge service. www.travelinsure.com/what/wmedhigh.asp

Pack-It system vacuum-sealed bags: These things are basically those plastic bags you see in commercials where they use a vacuum cleaner to suck all the excess air out of them. This model uses one-way valves; you simply put all your clothes inside and sit on them until all the air squishes out. I list these separately because even if you do not get the Pack-It system, you have to get these bags. They are unbelievable because they double the amount of usable space that you get in the same suitcase. Ideally, get two of them: one for clean clothing and one for dirty clothing. shop.eaglecreek.com/compression-sacs/l/214

Tripshell World Travel Adapter: The concept is pretty simple. This product offers one adaptor that allows you to charge your gear in any country regardless of what kind of outlets they are using. This one is great because it has a plug but a couple of adaptors for your Apple products all in one unit. On a side note, it is important to make sure that whatever appliances you are plugging in can handle the voltage for that particular country. www.amazon.com/dp/B005AF0C2G/?&tag=sherbent-20

SCOTTEVEST Travel Vest: The SCOTTEVEST vests and clothing are designed with many, many pockets in various places. Surprisingly though, you can only see two regular pockets. It allows you to carry your iPad and iPhone on a plane or around town and has pickpocket-proof places for your wallet, passport and other valuables. It's really hard to do this thing justice with just a written description. www.scottevest.com/

Micro Kickboard Luggage: It is really hard to describe how cool this thing is. Someone invented the carry-on hard case that has a scooter attached to it. That description probably makes it sound cheesy, but it's actually extremely cool. Once you're through security, the board and wheels that are flipped up into your luggage flip down, allowing you to stand on it and cruise through the airport at 10 or 15 miles an hour. It has a sleeve for a laptop and has to be the only luggage that comes with built-in transportation. I have given up on trying to describe this thing. www.microkickboard.com/luggage-scooters Here's a YouTube video of it in action. www.youtube.com/watch?v=LVN8AjM0T0s&feature=youtu.be

Visa HQ: This company takes all the guesswork and legwork out of getting a visa. Fill out a quick profile on their website, mail them your passport and a few snapshots and they do all they legwork for you. I had them get me eight visas at one time (one visa starts at $45) and it only cost me about $300. I highly recommend letting them do it for you. In my case, paying $300 beat the hell out of making trips to eight different embassies and standing in line roughly one zillion hours. www.visahq.com/

TripAdvisor: Once again this seems like a no-brainer, but they have some of the best reviews of places, and I have had great success using them. If you are not sure about a place based on the photos and reviews or are unsure about the area surrounding a resort you are about to book, just Google the name of the hotel and the words "trip advisor," and it will take you right to the review on that resort. www.tripadvisor.com/

Wikitravel: This site is basically Wikipedia, but for travel guides. You can pull up any city or country and get a host of basic information including attractions, transportation and links to other things for free. wikitravel.org/en/Main_Page

Semi-pro camera without the price tag: Sony NEX7: $650-$850
If you are going to start a travel blog and are not a serious photographer who is willing to haul a DSLR camera and 20 pounds of gear with you, check out the SONY NEX7. Its a new type of camera that is mirrorless, and it offers very similar results to a professional camera for a fraction of the price and size. It fits in your pocket and take photos close to 20 megapixels. It comes with a lens that shoot at F2, which means that you can take portrait that will look professional, and you can shoot in low-light situations like caves, old castles and churches.

I realize that technology changes so quickly that this camera will have be outdated within a few years. But mirrorless cameras are here to stay, and Sony has already started releasing even nicer versions that many pros are already using.

Travel insurance for all your camera gear and electronics: My brother and I bought an Globelink International insurance policy for one year on the website insuremygear.com. The policy gave us $25,000 of coverage and covered our laptops, iPads, camera gear and lenses, iPhones and all our other electronics. The policy covered anything other than throwing them into a volcano (literally, that's on the policy). It makes you wonder who was the person that ruined it for the rest of us by dropping their camera into a volcano. ☺

The policy covered theft, being submerged in water, breakage due to dropping them onto the ground, etc. It turned out to be a great investment because my brother managed to get his backpack stolen in Costa Rica with about $3,500 worth of stuff in it. His deductible was only $500. The claims process is actually quite easy. He just mailed a copy of his police report and his receipts for the items stolen, and they cut him a check within a couple weeks. www.globelink.co.uk

Mobile worldwide Internet: XCAM Global international Mifi rental Imagine a mobile hotspot for pretty much the entire world. ☺ The cost is a bit pricey (Global plans start at $395 a month) but if you need to stay connected for work, this may make traveling much easier for you. Here is a review: http://wavejourney.com/wj-reviews/data-internet-hotspot-xcom-global-international-mifi-rental-device.

No matter how sophisticated you may be, a large granite mountain cannot be denied – it speaks in silence to the very core of your being.
– Ansel Adams

Useful Travel Sites and Apps for the Advanced Traveler!

WWW.DROPBOX.COM
This website and app is especially helpful if you're going to travel for any extended period of time. On the road, there's always a chance that something could happen to your laptop. For about $10 a month, Dropbox will give you 100 gigs of online storage. This allows you to back up any of your important files from home such as your itinerary, copies of your passports and other important documents and put them online. It also allows you to store your photos that you're taking while traveling.

If you have insurance on your laptop and something were to happen, like theft or a little dunk in river, all you have to do is log back in and recover your most important files from Dropbox from anywhere with Internet connection. They also have an app to allow you to sync important files right from your iPhone. They will also give you a free account and the first 2 gigs of storage for free.

PACK & GO DELUXE
This app could not be any easier. You just click through a few folders and put checkmarks next to things you need to pack. When you are ready to go, click done on each item to take it off the list. Not only did the app work, it only took me 12 minutes to plan for a trip around the world. What's really convenient is that once you make a list, next time are ready to go, your packing list is, too.

TRIPIT

This is a super online travel organizer. Simply forward your itinerary via email to TripIt, who transfers it (over your data connection) into the phone for you. It can also put your hotel confirmations, and other information all in one spot. It works without an Internet connection so you can use it for free worldwide. If you lose your phone or computer, you can also log onto the website and post information from anywhere with Internet connection. (The intro video is hilarious – well worth the two minutes. www.tripit.com/uhp/learnMore)

KAYAK PRO

This is a good all around travel app and is the mobile version of the airfare search engine. You can use it to search all of the big travel websites at once. It can also convert currencies, organize your packing list, store an itinerary, look at airport maps, and a bunch of other things.

SKYPE

This Internet phone/video service just keeps getting better. The user interface is a lot like the iPhone now. You can keep your contacts in a Rolodex and call worldwide for a few cents a minute. It also supports video chat right on the phone. If you want to video chat with someone who does not have an iPhone, they can still use Skype from their computer. If you are not going to get an international cell phone while you're traveling, Skype is another option that can help. For small monthly fee you can also get your own Skype number that people can use to call you. You'll need to be logged on to Wi-Fi in order for the phone call to reach you, but if not online, they can still get your voicemail and leave you message.

AIRBNB

This site is a fantastic search engine for subletting condos, houses and apartments. The photos and overall design of the website is modern and makes you want to start packing your bags. They created guides to neighborhoods in major cities to help you understand the area will be staying in. They currently have 150,000 rooms in 190 countries. Are you headed out on vacation and live someplace that other people might be interested in going to? You can sublet your place while you're gone and use it to pay for your vacation!

LONELY PLANET GUIDEBOOKS AND APP

Lonely Planet is one of the foremost guidebook publishers and offers travel guides for destinations all over the planet. They have an excellent reputation for giving down-to-earth travel advice. You can buy these in person or you can buy them as apps and read them on your phone, saving you space and letting you take as many as you need for your entire trip.

TIME OUT

Time Out is a lot like an international version of Yelp. It shows you (location aware) contents such as the best places to eat, nightlife and entertainment.

STUCK ON EARTH

This one is a must-have iPad app for photographers or travelers. It shows you thousands of incredible images and exactly where they were taken. Even if you are not into photography, you will find tons of secret places by using this app and know exactly what they will look like before you go. It also allows you to retrace the photo walks of photographer Trey Ratcliff, so you can recreate his adventures.

PANO

For $2, this mobile app allows you to take great 180-360 photos, capturing the entire view you are seeing. It is great for ocean and mountain shots or vista with a much larger field of view.

UNESCO WORLD HERITAGE APP

This app shows you photos and information on the World Heritage sites and will add some places to your bucket list. It costs $5, but includes a list of over 900 awesome places, complete with 650 photos to get motivated.

EXPENSIFY

This app helps keep you on budget (super important) when traveling for months at a time. You can link your credit cards to it so that it will show you what your spending and you can scan receipts in case you have a way of using your travel as a write off when you get home. www.expensify.com

ZAGAT TO GO
Zagat is pretty much the Mercedes Benz of guidebooks for foodies. Any time you walk into a halfway decent place to eat, you may notice a little sign on the door that says, "Zagat Rated." If they put their name on it, is most likely a solid to excellent place to eat. The nice thing about this app is that you pay for one, but they give you 45 Zagat guides for different cities, making it like buying 45 guidebooks for the price of one. In my experience, Zagat is pretty spot on about their restaurant recommendations. Here is a link for Android users. If you have an iPhone, check the app store. www.zagat.com/mobile

APPS FOR FOODIES
www.theendlessweekend.com/tr

TRIPPY
This is a really cool app that is basically a vision board for your vacation dreams right on your phone or computer. Think of it as Pinterest for travel. You can organize images from places you've been and collect images of sites that you're dying to visit. It's also a great way to share images with others.

TRIP TRACKER LIVE FLIGHT STATUS TRACKER
Forget feeling flustered and lost in a new airport. This app will tell you flight status, arrival/departure terminal and gate info so you can get to your destination smoothly.

fourteen

10 Secrets To Surviving 24 Hours Of Flying

I learned the following tips the old fashioned way over the last few years.

#1: STEAL A BETTER SEAT

Some of the tips below can determine if you feel great or half dead after a long haul flight in coach. I discovered most of them out through flying myself and talking to other travelers.

If you can't afford business class or want to maximize your stack of miles, stay on your toes. As soon as the flight is in the air, all seats are fair game. If there is an entire row open, all you have to do is move. I have asked flight attendants if this is okay many times, and they have no issues with it.

Three seats with a couple of pillows and blankets are nearly as nice as first class. Even two seats are not a bad way to go. Lots of people will not have the courage to make a move like this, but they will look over with a bit of envy after they see you tucked in sleeping the flight away. I have noticed on the flights when I did not make this move myself that those seats always got filled within the first few minutes of the flight, so if they are getting filled anyway, you might as well enjoy the extra space for free.

Once you have set up shop, the key to getting comfortable is to take the seat belts and turn them sideways and wedge them in between the seats so that so you do not have them sticking you in the ribs while you're trying to sleep.

After that, use two blankets and three pillows to create a pillow tower. Use the final blanket to stay warm, and you just got a travel hacker upgrade to first class!

#2: Sleep Deeply with Melatonin

Melatonin is a natural hormone that your body produces to regulate your internal clock. It helps achieve a natural sleep when adjusting to a far-away time zone and reset your internal clock so you avoid have jet lag. Flight attendants often use it for this reason. You can buy 100 tablets over the counter for about $5 at drug stores and most grocery stores.

#3: The Relief Band

A small group of people can get motion sickness from flying. I lived in Puerto Rico for two years and had a 38-foot sailboat. My brothers and I would go sailing with four to six people for two to three days at a time. When things got rough, someone always got sick. To help ease the pain, I found a small electronic device that looks like a watch and stops motion sickness in about thirty seconds. It works perfectly. In fact, it works so well that the company stopped making ones with replaceable batteries and now only produces a disposable variety with a week of battery power. www.aeromedix.com/aeromedix_articles/reliefband/index.html

I recommend checking eBay and getting an original one with replaceable batteries. Thanks to this little device was able to deliver a 66-foot racing sailboat from St. Thomas to Fort Lauderdale. I made it through six days at sea without turning green.

#4: Become Super Hydrated

Hydration is key on long flights since you are breathing dry, recycled air. Skip the soda or wine and drink as much water as you can handle. I really can't say this enough; it is crucial. Often jet lag is really dehydration sickness.

Another neat shortcut to super hydration is to grab coconut water at the airport gift shop. Coconut water is so close to the makeup of your blood that it has been used in blood transfusions when there was no blood available. It helps prevent jet lag by making sure you have every mineral you need ahead of time.

#5: Avoid Heavy Foods Like the Plague

One of the worst feelings is to be stuck on an airplane with a horrible cramp. Also, according to a report from Associated Content, fatty foods and sugar can lower your immune system within ten minutes of their consumption. When flying long distance, you need an immune system firing on all cylinders. Examples of foods to avoid would be fried foods, pizza and basically any fast food.

There is an art, or rather a knack to flying. The knack lies in learning how to throw yourself at the ground and miss.
– Douglas Adams, Hitchhiker's Guide to the Galaxy

#6: Take a Yoga Break

I have gotten a few odd looks with this one, but it's totally worth it. If you have to choose between fitting in and being comfortable, I say go with comfort!

If you don't know any yoga stretches, simply find a quiet part of the airport (like an empty gate) and stretch your legs and arms. Massage your neck and shoulders, too. This helps stave off muscle spasms and knots and helps get your circulation going. It also helps prevent blood clots from forming due to lack of movement. If you already know yoga, do some basic poses and focus on your breathing for a while. Twenty minutes like this can reset your whole day and replace the pain caused by sleeping on a plane and traveling.

#7: Wear Comfortable Clothing and Shoes

Flying is no time to worry about looking nice (and hurting your feet) or to be sweating. Comfortable clothing will ensure you are well rested. Also, taking your shoes off from time to time helps.

#8: Use Earplugs or Noise Cancelling Headphones

Planes create massive sound frequency and electric fields. One way to reduce the noise effect is to block the sound. Why would an electrical field affect us? Your body runs on electricity. Seriously, you can measure the electrical field of your brainwaves with an EKG machine. Spending that much time next to an electrical field can throw your body off completely.

You can get a pair of the Bose noise cancelling headphones on eBay for about $150 (brand new they cost $300). They pretty much block all outside frequencies. If these are too bulky, they make an earbud version for about $150 new or you can always find a pair of good earplugs in most airport gift shops for about $5.

#9: Try a Light and Sound Machine

A light and sound machine is a small computer hooked to a pair of glasses and headphones. It uses light and sound frequencies to put you into a deep sleep or an energetic state. I know that it sounds crazy, but it works. The sleep program typically knocks me out in about ten minutes. The machine uses a technology called binaural beats to get your internal rhythm synced up and then speeds it up or slows it down. It feels kind of like a sound massage. Music uses the same principle.

I recommend Photosonix-Inner Pulse, which sells for about $179 with glasses and high-end headphones. A light and sound machine is perfect to pair up with a pair of the Bose headphones also. www.amazon.com/Photosonix-InnerPulse-Light-Therapy-Machine/dp/B000X2INLS

Need a cheaper alternative? If you have an iPhone, there are some applications that do this also. The experience is not quite as good, but it's still a very useful tool for quick relaxation.

#10: Endless Power Supply

Few things are worse than having no batteries on a long flight or layover. There is a super battery that will keep you going for days called HyperMac-External- Battery-for-iPad-iPhone-Mac. You can get one at www.hypershop.com. They have several different sizes starting at around $169. Even the basic model will recharge an iPhone 38 times on a single charge.

#11: Beat Jet Lag www.jetlagrooster.com

Part of beating jet lag on a new time zone is getting your body to eat and sleep on a schedule again. Someone designed a website to help you adjust your body's circadian rhythms, which are the 24 hour cycle you live on. You can help your body adapt in a few different ways. One of them is through exposure to light and dark and choosing when you eat. If you advance your circadian rhythm instead of reversing it, it is supposed to give you a much easier transition. You can find out exactly how to do this by going to the website above and putting in your flight schedule. It will send you a plan on exactly what to do. Here is a good article about it that explains it in more detail.

Special Report

The Secret to Skipping the Line in Customs and Security

Have you ever gotten stuck sitting in customs while trying to make a tight connection? How about running late at the airport and being stuck in a 30- minute security line while your flight is boarding and having to run through an airport with your luggage? I know I have had both of these rather stressful experiences many times.

What if I told you for $100 you could skip all that hassle for the next five years? Would you jump on that?

I recently put in an application to join a new group of travel elite that doesn't have to deal with any of that, and I am really excited about it, considering how much I fly.

Customs has a program called Global Entry. They provide kiosks at most airports in the U.S. and Canada that allow you to skip the customs line and just walk by a kiosk to check in with your passport. You scan your passport and do a finger scan and walk right through.

Once you are in Global Entry, you then can also use TSA Pre✓™, meaning you have been pre-screened and get your own line in security. Essentially once you are approved for Global Entry, you get a special trusted traveler number you give to the airline when booking your ticket. Once you give the airline this special number, they essentially upgrade your boarding pass to a golden ticket, allowing you to walk through like a superstar. In security, they put you into a special expedited line, which rarely has anyone in it.

Beside the fact that not many people get to use the "special line," it also moves much faster because you do not have to remove your shoes, take your approved liquids out, remove your laptop or your jacket or belt. Basically, you go back to pre-9-11 levels of security and walk through a regular old metal detector. They still reserve the right to do random checks, but I doubt you will see many of them.

I have talked to quite a few people that had gotten so frustrated dealing with security hassles at airports they had stopped traveling as frequently. Now for $100, you do not have to worry about it.

- Here is a link to the application for Global Entry: www.cbp.gov/travel/trusted-traveler-programs/global-entry

- Here is a link to info about TSA Pre✓™: www.tsa.gov/tsa-precheck/notification-tsa-precheck-eligibility

---

Once in a while it really hits people that they don't have to experience the world in the way they have been told to.
– Alan Keightley

fifteen

Location-Independent Nomads: Hacking The World Using Global Arbitrage

Imagine what it would feel like to have the absolute freedom to move to Spain for a month tomorrow or visit Hawaii or Argentina and stay as long as you liked without asking anyone's permission – all without having to find a new job while you are there because you're actually lowering your cost of living.

What if you could also fly for free when to get there because you had a healthy stack of miles in the bank? Imagine if you also had a free condo or flat or even a mansion to housesit in while you were there. When you start to combine a few of the chapters in this book, an entirely new type of nomadic adventure lifestyle becomes possible. Will it take some work? Absolutely, but no more work than going to school and working long hours at a job, which most people are able to accomplish.

If you think about what that might feel like, it is easy to understand why the mobile lifestyle and travel hacking can be so appealing. One word: Freedom!

If you start to connect some of these possibilities together, there really are entirely new levels of freedom available to the average person that have not ever really existed until this point in history. The Internet allows people to choose where they live and for how long.

There are few things that give a greater freedom than living anywhere you want, and in today's world, this is becoming easier by the day. If your job does not require you to physically be there, then the world is your oyster. Companies like www.homeaway.com have made feeling at home while you travel much more like home and house swapping and house sitting websites have made it possible to go for free if you're willing to put in a bit of time to learn the system.

When I am tired of staying in hotels, I will typically find a place for anywhere from a week to a month and rent an apartment or a flat somewhere. This saves you a ton of money in food costs and gives you most of the convenience of your own place. An apartment my brother rented in Amsterdam last year came even came with a bicycle and an umbrella.

My Twitter feed is full of people who move anywhere from once a week to once every few months. It completely depends on how much you like a place and how long you can get a visa for. You can stay in any eurozone country or combination of countries, for example, for 90 days with no questions asked. As long as you leave for 90 days you can come back and start over again for another 90. That is pretty much perfect if you time it the right way because the weather is only great in Europe about half of the time anyway. Many of the people I follow have started travel blogs that became successful and are using them to make a living, however many of them just do freelance work online and live wherever they feel like.

I have always wondered why birds stay in the same place when they can fly anywhere on the earth. Then I ask myself the same question.
– Harun Yahya

Literally millions of people make a living online these days. There are estimates that by 2020, roughly 50 percent of America's work force will work from home. Why wait? Home can be anywhere you want it right now.

The key is to watch out for the scams that will sap your enthusiasm. Unfortunately, the Internet is full of people trying to sell ideas on how to start a bunch of websites and get rich. That does not mean you cannot make money with a website, but there are lots of other ways to be a subcontractor these days and work online. What jobs, you ask? Pretty much anything that can be done on a computer.

There are many companies that will help you find work these days but one of the largest and best ones is Elance. www.elance.com.

Elance has around 500,000 contractors as of this publication. The number keeps changing, so as soon as I write, it will be outdated. For example, they added 180,000 new contractors in the first quarter of 2012 alone.

How much are people making? In the first quarter alone Elance paid out $43,000,000.

Web design and graphic design is big, but surprisingly 42 percent of the growth so far this year has been in the following:

- Video production
- Video editing audio editing
- Voiceover
- Writing
- Blogging

More companies are realizing that if you can do the work and they do not have to pay for office space, it is a win-win for everyone. Lots of people are going back to school right now, not even realizing that they could be holding the keys to complete freedom in their hands. I first found Elance while building my website. I hired someone to create logos for me.

The way it works is pretty simple. You put together a brief bio or folder on the type of work you want done. In my case, I wanted a logo. I wrote a brief description of my website and what I was looking for, and then I provided links to a few files that would give people inspiration. After that, designers dropped by and gave me quotes. Once I picked someone, my money went into escrow, so that on completion, the contractor was guaranteed to get paid.

CAN YOU REALLY MAKE ENOUGH MONEY TO TRAVEL CONSTANTLY?

This is where the global arbitrage comes in. If you speak English fluently and are from North America, you have a huge advantage in the freelance world. Even though someone may underbid you in India or China, many of the employers are coming from North America and they often would prefer to deal with someone from their continent. America hired more online contractors than any other country and was second only to India in staffing online positions.

The beauty of this is the way currency markets bounce around all the time. There are always some places that have great exchange rates. If you are making an average wage in America of say $30,000 to $40,000 a year but are living in Thailand, it goes much further. This means you get to work less and enjoy life more. When I was in Thailand last year, they had an hour of Thai massage for $10 in U.S. currency. That was in a resort area, which means the cost was about double what you would pay in most of Thailand. How well you live has nothing to do with how much money you make, but how far that money goes. After all, money is just a number, and it means nothing unless it gets you what you want.

Another way location-independent travelers use this concept of global arbitrage is to work in the more affluent countries and travel in the less expensive ones. This combination maximizes your resources, and if you try to buy local products and try to take excursions given by local companies, you are also contributing to the economy of the country that you are traveling in.

One of the best ways to learn almost any kind of software is through lydna.com.

They have full-length online classes on pretty much any Adobe software such as Photoshop, website building, and many other tutorials. There are 246 full courses on video editing, which is one of the top earners on Elance. You can learn any kind of software you want in a matter of weeks, and unlimited classes only cost $25 a month. Once you have skills, you put together a profile on Elance and you start off by bidding cheaply on things, after doing a few jobs and getting good feedback, you can raise the price you charge. I have often seen people making between $10-$60 a hour and even higher once they are well established.

Here is a great article on all kinds of ways you can continue to make money while traveling the world by Wandering Earl, who has been going non-stop for years. www.theendlessweekend.com/42_ways

If all of this seems like a good idea, here are two other good places to look for freelance work.

- www.odesk.com
  oDesk is one of the world's largest online marketplaces with over 500,000 businesses using them to hire online contractors.

- www.freelance.com
  Freelance has over $1 billion of projects posted that you can apply for right now. The possibilities are endless.

- www.regus.co.uk
  This membership is basically a one-stop shop for office space and printing shipping needs worldwide.

If you have a more traditional job you're doing while traveling and you need a place to work from, you can get it for free from this company. This can also be useful if you're traveling and you want to put yourself in a work environment separate from where you're staying. It sometimes helps to separate them.

The Business World Gold membership from Regus offers unlimited access to the business lounge in all of their locations worldwide (95 countries and counting), you can enjoy fast (and free) Wi-Fi Internet access, unlimited espresso machine use, and free printing and scanning services. Sometimes they will even let you use the private cubicles too, even though you are supposed to pay for them. If you need actual office space while you're traveling, they have plans for that also.

The membership costs $600 a year, but there are currently several ways to get free ones.

1. Go to the link below and enter the code. That will give you a free year to get started. If for some reason the code is no longer valid, try a quick Google search for "free Regus gold membership." Code: UKPFSB www.regus.co.uk/activate

2. Sign up for a Virgin Atlantic American Express card and you get the Gold Membership for life.

Business Support

If you want to learn online marketing or have a product to sell online, check out these two gurus.

Danny Iny from www.firepolemarketing.com
Danny has been called the Freddy Krueger of Blogging because when he first got started, he wrote so many guest posts it seemed like he was everywhere at once. He offers sage advice on marketing any product and building an audience from scratch.

Jeff Walker at http://jeffwalker.com
Jeff's students and clients have successfully helped launch 400 million dollars with of products using his methods. He has taught marketing to legends such as Tony Robbins among many others.

Both of these guys are expert online marketers and following them will give you an idea of what it will take to start a successful online business around a website. There are lots of other good online marketers out there, but these are two of the better ones, and they will be a good place to start if you are planning an online company.

I also highly recommend Scott Dinsmore from www.liveyourlegend.net. He is an expert at teaching people how to do work they love and follow their passion. Since I met him online, he has created a loyal following of 35,000 plus fans and recently gave a TED talk that quickly racked up nearly 2 million views. You can see it here: www.theendlessweekend.com/scott_d.

How To Teach English As A Ticket To Living Overseas

I first learned about this when a close friend of mine told me she had been hired to live in Rome, Italy for a month and teach English. She was given room and board and paid 500 euros 9 (which is about $700 U.S.) a week. I started looking into it, and there are hundreds, if not thousands, of opportunities like this in almost every country in the world.

You do not need to speak another language. In fact, they do not want you to so that you will not have any other choice but to speak English. If you want a longer-term experience in a country, you can teach English in a classroom. If you would like to just have a neat vacation experience, you can often stay with a family and do private tutoring for them. In this case, the family gives you room and board and you teach English for 15 hours a week. This seems like a great way to experience a culture and get a real feel for it. You eat whatever they eat and live the way they live and become part of the family for two to three months.

Some of the positions, if they are in schools or with executives for instance, may require a teaching certificate. Most of the in-home tutoring I discovered, however, will require nothing other than having English as your native language.

Be aware – there are some very extensive and somewhat expensive courses to become certified. Do your homework because while these may be a worthwhile option, there are also quite a few relatively inexpensive courses that may be all you need.

Here are a few sites to get you started:

- **InterExchange** www.interexchange.org
  They can also place you in working abroad programs such as au pair placements and help you get a visa and everything else you will need.

- **International Teacher Training Organization** – ITTO www.teflcertificatecourses.com
  This site along offers full certificates and guaranteed placement for life. Most schools apparently hire teachers with these certificates. The course lasts about six weeks and runs about $1,600. The neat thing about this option is that they host these courses all over the world, so the training itself is also a six-week adventure in another country.

There are many companies and websites out there that offer either certificates and jobs or simply jobs. There are way too many to list here, but a simple Google search for "teach English abroad" will give you pages of results. Just take your time and do your homework. Decide what kind of position you ultimately want and then decide if it is worth paying for a course or if you would rather just tutor with a family.

How to Hitchhike Around the World on Yachts!

My own experience with boats and sailing has taught me some lessons I will remember my whole life. My first foray into the boating world was at the age of 20. After living in the Caribbean for six months, I went back to Idaho and convinced my younger brother that we should return to the islands. The master plan was to buy a boat and drive it to Florida where we would sail it 1,000 miles to the Virgin Islands. Needless to say, at the time I did not know a lot about boating or offshore passages. I did, however, find someone crazy enough to let me put a 25-foot sailboat on layaway. It took us six months to pay it off, which shows you the state of sailboat sales in Idaho at the time that they were willing to accept such an offer. We finally got the boat, and after some lessons, we realized that it was not really seaworthy or safe for an actual ocean passage.

They say that the second-best day of a man's life is the day he buys a boat; beaten only by the day he sells it. We ended up moving to the islands without the boat, which was parked at my parents' house for the next eight years!

What I have learned is that what I really needed to get out on the water is not a boat, but sailing skills. There are so many ways to sail if you are a sailor, it is not even funny. Sailing is not just for boat owners because large boats require many people to sail them. I have friends that deliver yachts for a living all over the world.

I recently helped deliver a $5 million sailboat built out of carbon fiber from St. Thomas to Fort Lauderdale. The boat charters for $30,000 a week, but since I was part of the crew, I not only didn't pay a dime – they covered my expenses.

I have met countless sailors who have sailed around the world multiple times for free. Once you have a basic level of knowledge, it is as easy as going online and arranging to work for someone who is sailing from point A to B.

The best part of delivering boats and crewing for a living is that you can get paid to travel, or at least get some of your expenses covered. Once you have the skill set you can literally show up at a marina and hitch-hike your way all over the world. You eat for free and have a place to live on the boat – what else do you need? ☺

How do you start yacht-hopping and what are the easiest ways to find a boat to work on?

The starting point is getting several sailing certifications, which are the sailing equivalent of a driver's license. ASA is the organization that does most sailing training in the states. Getting the first three certifications will run somewhere around $2,000 and will take about six weeks. The school I went to allowed my brother and I both to get certified for $2,000 if we took the classes together.

Once you knock this out, you can legally go charter any boat up to 50 feet and take it out on the ocean overnight. While this is not the end of your learning process, it is enough so you can handle duties as a crewmember and pull your own weight. If you can't afford to spend the money, another great way to start is by finding a local sailing club and volunteering at whatever regattas they host.

This way you can to learn about sailing for free, and racing is an intense environment that will shorten the learning curve! The great thing about sailors is that they are more than willing to share their knowledge and love of sailing. Sailors are a rowdy and sarcastic bunch, so be willing to take your fair share of licks as you learn.

Once you have the skill set, finding a boat that needs help is the easy part. Even without the any skills at all, if you are willing to learn and have a great attitude, you may find a spot. Boats move with the seasons. In the fall, they are headed for the Caribbean, and in the spring, they are headed for the Mediterranean, as an example. All it takes to get a ride is to respond to ads of people looking for crewmembers. You can find links to some of them on the Endless Weekend website or by doing a simple Google search. Your duties will consist of helping sail the boat and keeping it in good shape while being delivered. Everyone will most likely take turns cooking and cleaning also.

If you are interested in owning a boat, try checking out the many companies like SailTime (www.sailtime.com) that now offer boat timeshares. My brother and I owned a timeshare on a 38-foot sailboat when I lived in Puerto Rico, and it was amazing. The cost is between $400 to $800 a month, depending on the number of days you want to sail. In our case we spent about $450, and we had a 38-foot boat between four to six days a month. We used it to sail over to other islands up to several days at a time. It slept six people and was equipped with a GPS and autopilot as well as a Bose surround sound system and television.

One of the things high on my bucket list is to spend a month or two on a tall ship. There are hundreds of tall ships still in action and many of them do perpetual circumnavigations of the world.

What is a tall ship? Think *Pirates of the Caribbean*! They are multi-mast boats, up to several hundred feet long, that can require as many as 100+ crewmembers. One I have been following for a while now is called Picton Castle. It is 400 feet long and has circled the earth multiple times.

Anyone can join as a crewmember in six-week increments, and everyone pays their share of expenses to keep the boat going. This is one of the examples where it may be worth it to spend some money on the experience. Last time I checked, it was around about $800 a week. Imagine pulling into some faraway port in a 400-foot long pirate ship with 100 of your new best friends, ready to take over the town! It may not be for everyone, but if this sounds like your idea of heaven, it is so much easier than you think.

sixteen

The Secret Facebook Hack You Need to Know

How use three degrees of separation to meet friends, and see the world.

There are few better things than going to an exotic or difficult destination and getting the local hookup. We all have had this experience at one time or another, when we stayed with a friend or family member in a new place and they showed the best spots to eat, the secret places the tourists miss and introduced us to neat people we would never have met otherwise.

How is it possible to create this type of experience on purpose without actually knowing someone at the destination?

Easy. Learn how to make friends over social media at places you want to go to. This may sound like a simplistic answer, however the devil is in the details.

My brother has become the master of this. Lots of people have a thousand people on their Facebook friends list, but very few of them manage to create a unique and positive impression that last with all of them. He creates such great connections with people that he gets invitations for all sorts of adventures.

I have seen my brother couch surf around the world for several months at a time and hardly touch a hotel or youth hostel. He found places to stay everywhere from Valencia, Spain to the French Riviera and other places you think would be impossible, like the mountains of Patagonia in Chile.

Most of the places he visited where he did stay in a hotel or hostel, he at least knew someone in advance and went out and partied with the locals.

So how exactly does he do this?

Here are three simple steps to the worldwide networking.

THE NEW LAW OF SEPARATION: THREE DEGREES, NOT SIX

We all have heard about the six degrees of separation. Well, that was before social media, and the average person only knew 200 people. The Internet has rewired the world and the way connections work. In most cases, you can find someone that knows someone in almost any other country in with only two degrees and always with three.

So how do you actually put this into practice?

STEP 1:

Start treating your social media more like a place to meet interesting people and not a place to spam random controversial topics. In other words, show people things that benefit them or are interesting to the majority of people and things that do not upset 50 percent of the population. This means skip religion and politics and any of those stupid Facebook games or chain letters. Anyone with high standards will hide your posts if they are negative, political or highly critical of other people's religious or life views.

If you are meeting someone online for the first time, you have to put your best foot forward. No one wants to introduce a cool international friend to someone and then regret it.

Carefully go through your Facebook page and delete any photos or posts that could make you look like or sound like an idiot. We all have had them at one time or another. Assume people you are trying to network with are going to go through this page when deciding if you are interesting and cool or not.

Once you have done that, delete photos that are redundant or too similar. One of the biggest differences between a horrible photographer and an amazing one is not always ability. The difference is that a really good photographer only posts the one percent of their photos that are really good while most people post all of them. Most people do not want to see 150 photos of your excursion to the museum – we just want to see the four or five awesome ones.

When you post every photo on your camera, people will look at the first few until they start to look redundant or they see some bad ones, and then they move on to something else. If your good ones are mixed in with a bunch of ones that should be in the reject pile, chances are no one will ever see the best ones you took. Keep the standards high; they will want to keep on looking because each one is interesting.

STEP 2:

Let's say you want to meet someone cool in France and are planning on going in 90 days. You have about 200 friends on your Facebook page. You simply do an occasional post and ask, "Does anyone know anyone in Paris? I am going to be there this summer, and I would like to meet interesting people." If you do not get a response, ask a few of your closest friends to do a similar post for you.

Think about how big the numbers get if you go out two to three degrees from you. If each person only had 200 people on their Facebook account it would look like this:

One degree of separation equals 200 x 200 = 40,000. This means that if you have access to 200 people and the 200 people they have access to, you are looking at 40,000 people.

Here is where it gets crazy, though. If went out one more degree, which means a friend of a friend's friend, you are looking at access to 8,000,000 people.

This can be as easy as just asking, "Hey, does anyone know someone in Rio or anywhere else in Brazil? If not, do you happen to know someone that knows someone?" That is literally all it can take to get access to up to 8,000,000 people.

STEP 3:

After you have a cool page and you have gotten an introduction or recommendation, you simply send a friend request with a personal message.

Try something like, "I am a friend with George, and he thought maybe we ought to be friends." You do not even need to get into the fact you are heading for Rio in 90 days.

Once they accept your friend request, make sure you start to pay attention to their news feed. Comment on their posts and like the stuff you find interesting. Organically start conversations and start to develop a friendship. Once that has happened, point out that you are going to be in their neck of the woods and ask if they have would be interested in hitting the town. Ask if they know of any inexpensive places to stay or if they might have a spare bedroom they would want to rent out for cheap for the week.

You would be amazed at what life will hand you if you are just willing to ask for it. I am constantly amazed at the insanely awesome places my brother keeps landing in, and I have started to join him in his version of social couch surfer.

Breathe. Let go. And remind yourself that this very moment is the only one you know you have for sure.
– Oprah

---

seventeen

How To Avoid Getting Sick, Frustrated Or Burned Out On A Long Travel Stint

There are a few ways to ruin your travel experience when you are traveling for months at a time. One of them is to not have the mental and emotional balance to deal with unforeseen problems. It could mean a missed flight or a bad hotel room; it could be injuring yourself or getting sick. Any rough experience can take the fun out of a trip.

One of the easiest ways to stay grounded and grateful when these things come up is to create balance before they happen. Yoga is one of the easiest and most beneficial ways to combat all of the above. It keeps your muscles loose and body in alignment after sitting on buses, planes or trains.

Yoga lowers your stress levels so you can stay calm and choose the right approach when unforeseen things happen. Many injuries occur because a person's muscle system is so full of knots and tension that is easy to pull a muscle or strain your back. Traveling long term can also lower your immune system if you are not supporting our health. Between jet lag and eating in airports and not knowing your way around new and sometimes exotic cuisines, I have seen many people get colds and serious illnesses when they are not doing something to balance out the extra stress they are putting on themselves.

Yoga helps support your body so you can prevent many common problems while traveling. First of all, yoga is a great way to continue to get exercise while traveling. Many people think of yoga as similar to meditation and are unaware what an amazing workout it can be. It engages your entire body and really gives you the strength to move your body however it is needed.

Sitting on a long flight can give you all sorts of kinks and knots but 5- to 10- minute yoga stretch sessions while waiting for your next flight can make you feel like a new person. You are just going to be sitting there anyway, so why not indulge in a little relaxation and enjoy your next flight more?

YOGA TRAVEL TIPS

- While on the road, there are several ways to continue taking classes. One of the best is to go track down a class wherever you end up. This can be a great way to meet interesting people from the area.

- Yogadownload.com is a subscription website that allows you to take virtual classes online on your laptop and download them for a time when you do not have an Internet connection.

- Buy some DVDs to rip into your computer or download some audio yoga classes. If you have never done yoga before, the DVDs will be easier. I highly recommend David Swanson. His classes are amazing, and he makes it really easy to follow. You can start by using his DVDs and then also download the audio, so if you get stuck in an airport, you can simply turn on his 15-minute routine on your iPod for a great stretching session.

- At the end of just 15 minutes, you will feel like a new person. It is a lot like going for a run and getting a nice massage afterwards.

Last but not least, if you happen to be single, you will find yoga classes worldwide to be an excellent place to meet new friends and attractive people. Timothy Ferriss, author of 4-Hour Workweek, once said that if you just moved to a new country and want to make new friends, just go pick up any team sport, especially one you do not know how to play. When you leave the field, you will have more friends than you can shake a stick at. You will often find yoga and dance classes to be the same way.

The secret of health for both mind and body is not to mourn for the past, worry about the future, or anticipate troubles, but to live in the present moment wisely and earnestly.
- Buddha

ZEN TRAVEL

As often happens in life, one of my greatest mistakes led me to a new path. The path was always there and even though I always knew of it, knowing it and walking down it are never the same thing.

Ever since I could remember, I felt called to a life of adventure and exploration. I wanted to see the world and experience every amazing thing I could. As a kid, I read countless books on exploration and people who set out into the world to have great adventures. I ran away to the Caribbean with only $300 in my pocket when I first turned 18 and lived on a beach until I could start a new life there. At the age of 33, I decided it was finally time that I take my first long-term trip around the world.

To make a long story short, I did take my trip around the world, and it was amazing. But even though I saw some of the most wonderful things in the world, I did not fully turn off the drive that it had taken me to get there. My mind needed to have goals and kept me moving forward constantly which kept me from fully living in the present moment. When I got home I realized that I had some how missed part of what I had set out to do, which was to fully absorb every detail and emotion and connection that the world could offer me.

What exactly had I missed and why?

There are states of bliss that a very small group of people live in that the average person does not often experience. Travel, for many of us, has the ability to put us in to a childlike state of wonder and enthusiasm. When we are confronted with something so stunning we forget to think about anything else than the current moment, the power of joy, bliss and happiness that actually is our natural state of being gets the opportunity to come through us with the power of the universe behind it.

In the book *The Alchemist*, the shepherd Santiago meets a king who understands happiness. He asks the king to tell him the secret. The man gives him a spoon with two drops of oil and asks him to walk around his house for two hours. When the boy returns, the king asks him how he enjoyed all of the incredible art and sculptures all over his palace. The boy looked at him in surprise and said that he was so busy making sure he did not drop the oil, he hadn't noticed.

The king tells the boy to go walk around again for two hours and this time, to notice everything around him. The boy walked around this time in awe at the beauty that surrounded him. When he returned, he walked in a state of bliss and joy at the marvels he had just seen. This time, the king asked him about the oil. The boy suddenly realized that he must have dropped it somewhere. The secret to success and joy, the king told him wisely, is noticing everything around you without dropping the oil.

Life is exactly like this story. Travel is by far one of the greatest chances to see the treasure all around us. It can take a lot of juggling of money and planning to actually get there, so it is important to make those things happen first. However, the joy comes from seeing the world with a new set of eyes and feeling connected to all the incredible beauty of each moment you find yourself in.

So what does this state of bliss feel like?

I can only explain my experiences with it, but there is a quiet and stillness that one can achieve where for a time you do not think about anything other than the moment you are experiencing right now. The feel of the earth under your feet, the kiss of the wind on face, the vibration of the sounds in the air as it enters your ears. The more we let go of whatever we have been through and whatever we are planning in the future, the better we feel about what is happening right now.

A child can experience a state of bliss when they find a seashell for the first time. As an adult, you can do the same thing anytime you want to; it's just that most people are too busy letting their mind go crazy worrying about things that either already happened or might happen someday that we don't let ourselves feel it.

The first time I experienced this state of being fully present it was so profound that I felt like I was seeing the world for the first time. The colors were brighter, the sounds were sweeter, I looked around at the world in such a state of awe I ended up with a huge silly grin on my face.

How exactly does one attain this? In the information age, we are so used to being bombarded with stimuli that the average person rarely experiences this sort of peacefulness and calm. Like all things, it is a matter of practice. The good news is that it's something you can practice at anytime you are awake.

When you make dinner at your house there are two ways you can do it. The first one is to make dinner as a chore or something to hurry through so you can get on with your life. The second one is to make dinner and actually make dinner. That is to enjoy every smell and sensation while you do it. Notice the colors of the vegetables and think only about each current moment that you are in, since after all, that moment is the only one you can ever truly have.

In the Adam Sandler movie *Click*, the main character gets a remote control and unwisely uses it to fast forward past moments of his life he thinks are not peak experiences. By the end of the movie, he realizes he missed his entire life. By always looking somewhere else other than right now, this current moment, he didn't feel all the love, joy, passion and bliss that were right at his fingertips.

The easy way to come back to the present, no matter what else is happening, is to simply start by focusing on your breath. The breath is the connecting point between your mind body and soul. It brings you into the current moment and allows you to start it. Once you have started with your breath, then extend your awareness out to your physical body and check in with yourself and see how you are feeling. Notice your thoughts, but let them drift by you and realize you are not your thoughts or your feelings. The better you get at this, the faster you realize the only thing that prevents us from experiencing peace and bliss in any moment is the chatter that happens in our own inner monologue.

Someone once asked Buddha if he was a god, and Buddha said, "No, all I am is awake." Being truly awake and present in this life is so rare that it may seem like a superhuman feat at times, however nothing is further from the truth. Not only can any person become more awake, but being awake is our natural state of being, and it is only the constant clutter of our thoughts and emotions, our fears and our desires that stops us from experiencing this natural state of mind at any time.

A great book that illustrates this is *The Miracle of Mindfulness* by Thich Nhat Hanh. The book is extremely easy reading and gives you simple ways to enjoy a state of mindfulness and bliss in everything you do. It does not spend a lot of time on philosophy or religion but is a simple how-to guide. Imagine experiencing joy even in the most seemingly mundane things such as cleaning your house. If this sounds interesting, this book is worth your time.

Perhaps travel cannot prevent bigotry, but by demonstrating that all peoples cry, laugh, eat, worry, and die, it can introduce the idea that if we try and understand each other, we may even become friends.
– Maya Angelou

---

eighteen
Open Your Heart, Give Back To The World

What if you could save the world just a little bit while you are out there exploring it?

Travel can often afford us a chance to make a big impact for a fraction of what we could do it for at home. Obviously, you can make a difference wherever you are, but in some poorer countries, a tiny bit of money can go a long way. It is also a way to connect with your own gratitude while seeing the world. You will be surprised to see how even attempts to make a small difference with the people you meet on the road will repeatedly come back to you. You can also use changing the world as a means of low-cost traveling through volunteer programs.

*Thousands of candles can be lit from a single candle,
and the life of the candle will not be shortened.
Happiness never decreases by being shared.
– Buddha*

Warren Buffett likes to talk about the ovarian lottery. He offered the following scenario:

It's 24 hours before your birth, and a genie appears to you. He tells you that you can set the rules for the world you're about to enter — economic, social, political — the whole enchilada. Sounds great, right?

What's the catch?

Before you enter the world, you will pick one ball from a barrel of 7 billion, the number of people on the planet. That ball will determine your gender, race, nationality, natural abilities, and health — whether you are born rich or poor, sick or able-bodied, brilliant or below average, American or Zimbabwean.

For every 100 balls in the jar, five would be from America. Out of those five, half would be men and half would be women. Out of those, half would have a below-average IQ. Some would be from good homes, and some wouldn't be. He always asks the question, "If given the chance, would you roll the dice, or do you feel grateful for the lottery ticket you pulled?"

That said, we all have a lot to be grateful for, we could have been born 150 years ago when this kind of travel was impossible.

THE GIRL IN AGRA

One of the best ways to express gratitude on the road is by taking good care of at least some of the people you are going to meet along the way. While in India, Marie, a good friend of mine who is a nurse, was in a taxi and passed through a very poor neighborhood in Agra, not far from the Taj Mahal. The cab driver stopped as many homeless children came up to the car, and one particular girl caught my friend's eye. She had a badly infected hand to the point where she could easily have lost it if she was not treated with antibiotics soon.

My friend sadly only had a small amount of cash on her, but she was so struck by the girl's situation that she went to get more cash and gave it to the girl. It turned out that the cost of a doctor's visit and antibiotics only cost about $6.

Can you imagine such a small amount of money standing between you and missing one of your hands for the rest of your life? There can be many opportunities like that on the road if you embrace them, and the people you help will not be the only ones who benefit. If you do this from a place of desire to help others, you will experience happiness on your journey that not many people find.

The irony is that the richness you can take away from an experience like that and the perspective you can take back into your regular life is huge. When you make a contribution to someone who really needs it, you will also be changed by the experience.

Many times when we are caught up in our own needs we can miss opportunities like this even if they are all around us. The person driving your cab can be another example.

One of my other friends, while in traveling in a poorer country, started talking to his cab driver and asking how much he paid for various things in life, such as his rent and other living expenses. My friend's goal was simply to understand someone else and their struggle. What he discovered was quite amazing. He found that his driver was having a very hard time coming up with the money to put his daughter into school the next year. After a week of great service, my friend gave him a tip for $200, which was enough to cover tuition for his daughter for the entire year. I am not sure who benefited from that exchange more, my friend or the cab driver. The whole experience brought them both to tears.

These types of moments will stay with you in a way that many of the touristy things you see and do may not. I am not telling you to skip seeing the mystical monuments of the world, but when you are in a cab and on the way there, take time to peer down the alleys and walk down the side streets. See the way people are really living and the raw and uncensored life away from the tourist trail.

It's not a secret, but more a must. When traveling, seek to get to know the local people and truly understand what their life is like. You don't need to walk a mile in their shoes, but walking a few steps each place you go will not only increase your knowledge about the world and the human condition, but also your empathy toward all of mankind. Living and eating with locals will save you money and forge new friendships. The biggest cost of long-term travel is maintaining your level of comfort in far-flung places. If you can get comfortable with less comfort, you'll have far richer experiences in the end.

Adam Pervez, http://www.HappinessPlunge.com

Make a difference and save money at the same time

If you want to go full out with this concept, you can also combine volunteering while you travel. Not only can it bring your travel costs down, but it also will put you into situations and help you meet people that you would never see otherwise. Many organizations offer volunteering vacations where you are housed, fed and given some time to see the sites. In exchange, you give your time to a project that serves the community. These are really affordable ways to get out and see the world and make it a better place at the same time.

If you would like to do a volunteer vacation, check out these places to get started.

- **Volunteer HQ** www.volunteerhq.org
  Packages for a full week started at an average of $180 to $300 for a full week, including accommodations. They offer placement in countries such as Thailand, China, Brazil, Nepal, Costa Rica and Peru to name a few.

- **World Teach** www.worldteach.org
  If you would like to try something more substantial like volunteering and living in another country for the summer or even the

year, this company offers packages for $4,995 for an entire year! Imagine living in Tanzania or Ecuador for a year for $4,995.

- **Globe Aware** www.globeaware.ca
  Focuses on one-week trips for the volunteer traveler who cannot afford to take lots of time off. For example, they have a 1-week trip to Cuba that includes mid-range hotels, food local transportation and lots of other help for one week for $1,650.

- **Vaops** www.vaops.com
  This NGO offers completely free and low-cost opportunities to volunteer abroad.

- Both www.umabroad.umn.edu and www.volunteerinternational.org Offer advice on selecting the right volunteer programs for you.

USE TRAVEL TO REINVENT YOURSELF!

Travel – especially the long-term kind – can be a profound tool for reshaping yourself into someone completely different. It has the power to melt away old beliefs systems. It gives you new perspective and introduces you to entirely new ways of eating, dressing, thinking - about just about everything else we take for granted as the "correct" way of doing things.

There are, of course, countless tourists that never have any of these experiences, who go home the same people they were when they started. I admit that I have been guilty of this sheltered approach at times. When you pay attention and live in the moment though, you will have some of the most incredible experiences life can offer.

Have you ever considered who you actually are? If I asked who you are, what would you say? Would you say that you are an American, or a husband or a dentist? Are you those things? They are things you do or things you may believe in, but none of them are who you are.

We are much more than are beliefs or are needs in life. We are more than our emotions or the roles we take on in our relationships or our jobs. All of these things, if you know how, can be changed as easily as we change clothing. Travel offers us that chance to take a fresh look at who we are by not only gaining new perspective on where we have come from, but also because we cannot rely on our usual assumptions. No one you meet has any history with you or expectations of who you have to be. You can be anyone you want and reinvent yourself as much as you want.

LIFE IS NOT ABOUT FINDING YOURSELF; IT IS ABOUT CREATING YOURSELF

Every chance to see a new country and culture is also a chance to look at your own way of life and see what about it you truly love and what you might like to do differently. Living in the Caribbean helped me really appreciate American infrastructure, but it also helped me notice that as a group, Americans are not the happiest culture. In fact, in many happiness surveys, we have ranked near the bottom. There are some things that we do really well in this country and others that we do not do well at all. So my question is, how can you know that the way of life you were handed is the best one for you without going out and trying some other ones? At least experience some new possibilities for a few days at a time. You can always take what you like and leave what you don't.

As in most things in life, fear is often the main thing that holds people back from their dreams. After taking my first trip around the world, I can honestly say there are very few places I am afraid of visiting. That does not mean that you should not do your research and be prepared. However, eight times out of ten, whatever negative press we see about a place is hyped up to boost ratings.

I was in Egypt in 2011 right after the Egyptian people overthrew their government, and not only did I not have any problems, but everyone was very welcoming. I was also in Greece during the protests in Athens and watched some of the protests myself. If you watched the news, you might have thought the entire city was a war zone. Yet only two blocks from Syntagma Square where angry crowds were protesting, people were enjoying nice desserts at outdoor cafes and talking with each other. When the press is really bad, travel to these locations goes on sale. I stayed in a 5-star hotel in Athens that is normally about $600-800 a night for $200 a night because of the bad press. You often will find that each fear you conquer in life opens up new doorways of possibility and opportunity.

Traveling allows us to experience the magic of destiny or coincidences in a whole new way. There is a magic that happens when you are outside of your comfort zone, yet open to whatever experience lands in your lap. Travel is one of the easiest ways to connect and have spontaneous adventures.

I was in Costa Rica and walking up a dirt road to a festival with my brother Nathaniel. Right as we walked up to the shuttle stop for a ride into the festival, the shuttle pulled away. My brother and I smiled to each to other instead of being upset and started walking.

At that exact moment a local man came galloping by on a horse pulling a string of horses behind him. He seemed to appear almost out of thin air. He looked at us and shouted, "Pura vida!" which means "pure life" in Spanish. We shouted it back to him "Pura vida!" and I put my hand up at the same time. He stopped his entire string of horses, and we ran up and jumped on two of them. He let the ropes loose and galloped off, leaving us with two fresh horses to ride to the festival on our own. It was a moments of pure spontaneous magic that was hard to describe.

I had never met this man, yet he just handed me two horses and left without saying more than "Pure life!" and smiling. Little moments like these, where the normal somehow becomes magical, are one of the best reasons to break out of your comfort zone and go have the adventure of your life.

Until we meet on the road, I wish you luck in all your adventures. You can always find me at www.theendlessweekend.com. Feel free to say hello or send me your questions or ideas on making this book more effective.

I would love to hear your feedback at theartofworldtravel@gmail.com.

Not all who wander are lost.

– Justin

APR 05 2016

Made in the USA
Charleston, SC
19 March 2016